P9-BYH-737

rachael, ray's
look+cook

rachael, ray's
look✛cook

100 can't-miss main courses in pictures

+ 125 more **ALL-NEW** recipes: interactive 30-minute meals, sides, sauces & yum-o menus!

photographs by stephen murello

Clarkson Potter/Publishers
New York

Copyright © 2010 by Rachael Ray
The illustrations that appear in chapter 5 originally
appeared in *Yum-O!* and *Every Day with Rachael Ray,*
copyright © Chris Kalb.
Food photography shot in natural light by Stephen Murello,
copyright © 2010 by Stephen Murello
Photograph on page 11 by Jim Wright, copyright © 2010
by Jim Wright

All rights reserved.
Published in the United States by Clarkson Potter/Publishers,
an imprint of the Crown Publishing Group, a division of
Random House, Inc., New York.
www.crownpublishing.com
www.clarksonpotter.com

CLARKSON POTTER is a trademark and POTTER with
colophon is a registered trademark of Random House, Inc.

Library of Congress Cataloging-in-Publication Data
is available upon request

ISBN 978-0-307-59050-3

Printed in the United States of America

Design by Amy Sly

10 9 8 7 6 5 4 3 2 1

First Edition

this book is dedicated to
those with big appetites
for life & for food

look ✛ cook recipes

more recipes!

acknowledgments

Thank you to Wes "BB" Martin, Lovely Leslie Orlandini, and the whole team of food stylists who helped me take thousands of pictures over dozens of days so we could create a foolproof recipe collection. Thanks to Stephen Murello and his assistant, Greg Morris, who shot in time-consuming but soooo rich-looking natural light. My food has never looked quite so delicious.

Thanks to my loving family, husband, and dog, who test-stomach each recipe.

Thanks to Abigail Bodiker, Kara Vogt, Patrick Decker, Jorge "Papi" Andrango, Jeanette Donnarumma, and Emily Rieger for the delicious devotion and dessert tutelage.

Thanks to Michelle Boxer, who is my hero and who unscrambles my runny-egg brain each day. Thank you to Kappy the Kapster Andrew Homeslice Kaplan, for helping edit this book and for being a food guru and my personal dining guide.

Thank you to Emily Takoudes, Peggy Paul, and Lauren Shakely for helping me provide a completely unique cookbook that is the best possible value. You really help me give my readers the most bang for their buck. Also thank you to Amy Sly, Jane Treuhaft, Marysarah Quinn, Derek Gullino, and Amy Boorstein.

And as always thank you to our viewers and readers; I wouldn't have any of my many jobs without you. Hope you love the Look ✚ Cook as much as I do.

introduction
yes, you can!

The theme of all of the work I do remains the same today as it was the day I wrote my first 30-Minute Meal more than fifteen years ago: Anyone and everyone can cook a good meal. You do not need special skills or an exorbitant budget to prepare good-quality food for yourself or others. Good food and fine living are not reserved for the rich. Having a rich quality of life can be as accessible as a simple supper and a positive state of mind.

The Look + Cook 100 are as foolproof as recipes can get. This collection of recipes is the paint-by-numbers of food preparation. In each of the Look + Cook 100 you can see and study each step of each entrée as it is being prepared. In some cases, a recipe is not even necessary; you can see the ingredients and the amounts clearly represented. But the recipes are here for you, too, along with the same freehand style of teaching method that I always use.

Each recipe can be served as is or with a simple salad; but many of the recipes, especially those designed for entertaining, have suggested starters or side dishes as accompaniments and they are cross-referenced throughout the book. There are even a few easy desserts to choose from, although I must confess that when dinner guests offer to bring something I take them up on it. "Bring sweet treats, please!"

The Look + Cook 100 are divided into three categories: Cozy Food, Make Your Own Takeout, and Fancy Fake-Outs. Don't let the labels stop you from entertaining with recipes from any of the three sections. I feel that entertaining with comfort foods or takeout-style casual foods can often place your guests more at ease and result in dinner parties that have more life than fancy sit-down celebrations—although for date nights and special occasions you need a few easy yet elegant entrées in your repertoire.

Whether you cook five nights a week and could write a book of your own or you have been too intimidated to ever pick up a chef's knife, the Look + Cook 100 will have your back literally every step of the way from kitchen to table.

LOOK + COOK RECIPES

1 cozy food

Comfort foods make you feel cozy from the inside out. These meals, like Spinach and Artichoke Mac 'n' Cheese on page 42 and Turkey Chili Shepherd's Pie with a Sweet Potato Topper on page 19 are feel-good favorites. I make cozy meals for myself or for my family at the end of especially long days, on nights when I feel a cold coming on, or when we are in need of a little cheering up at our house. Cozy foods are extra-delicious on cold nights, eaten by a crackling fire or curled up under your favorite blankie. Feel better. Make dinner tonight.

2 make your own takeout

3 fancy fake-outs

caesar spaghetti

SERVES 4

Salt

1 pound spaghetti **or whole-wheat or whole-grain spaghetti**

¼ cup EVOO (extra-virgin olive oil), **plus some for drizzling**

6 to 8 anchovy fillets, **drained**

4 large garlic cloves, **grated or finely chopped**

2 teaspoons Worcestershire sauce **(eyeball it)**

2 medium heads of escarole, **washed and dried**

Lots of coarse black pepper

¼ teaspoon freshly grated nutmeg, **or to taste**

1 lemon

2 large egg yolks

1½ cups grated Pecorino Romano **cheese**

Bring a large pot of water to a boil for the pasta. When the water boils, add salt and cook the pasta to just shy of al dente. Heads up: You need to reserve about 1 cup of starchy cooking water just before draining. ■ While the pasta is cooking, place a large skillet over medium-high heat with the EVOO. Add the anchovies to the pan and cook until they've melted into the oil, about 2 minutes. Reduce the heat to medium-low and add the garlic. Stir for 1 minute, then add the Worcestershire sauce. Tear the escarole and add several handfuls at a time, then stir the wilting greens to coat with the garlic oil. Season the greens with lots of pepper and a little nutmeg, then squeeze the juice of the lemon over the greens. ■ In a heat-proof bowl, add the reserved pasta cooking water to the egg yolks and beat together to temper them. Turn off the heat under the skillet and toss the drained pasta with the greens and eggs and half of the cheese to coat evenly; toss vigorously for 1 minute. Dress the mixture with an extra drizzle of EVOO and serve. Pass the remaining cheese at the table.

For a super starter to this menu try the **Spinach Salad on Garlic Croutons** (page 266).

turkey chili shepherd's pie
with a sweet potato topper

Place the potatoes in a large pot, cover with cold water, and bring to a boil. Salt the water and cook until tender, 12 to 15 minutes. Drain and return the potatoes to the hot pot, then mash with the butter, orange zest, and crème fraîche or sour cream. Season with salt, pepper, and nutmeg to taste. ■ While the potatoes are coming to a boil, heat a chili pot with the EVOO over medium-high to high heat. Add the turkey and brown, breaking up the meat, then add the onion and cook for 2 to 3 minutes while you chop the chile peppers, bell pepper, and garlic. Add the peppers and garlic to the pot, season with the spices, salt, and black pepper, and cook for 8 to 10 minutes more. Stir in the tomato paste for 1 minute, then add the stock and simmer for a few minutes longer to thicken and combine the flavors. ■ Preheat the broiler. ■ Place the chili in a casserole dish, spread the mashed sweet potatoes on top, and cover with the cheddar cheese. Brown under the broiler until golden.

SERVES 4 to 6

2½ **pounds** sweet potatoes
(4 or 5 potatoes), peeled and cubed

Salt

4 **tablespoons (½ stick)** butter,
cut into pieces

2 **teaspoons grated** orange zest

1 **cup** crème fraîche **or sour cream**

Black pepper

Freshly grated nutmeg, **to taste
(about ¼ teaspoon)**

2 **tablespoons EVOO (extra-virgin
olive oil)**

2 **pounds** ground turkey

1 **large** onion, **chopped**

2 **small** chile peppers, **such as
Red Fresno, jalapeño, or serrano**

1 red bell pepper, **seeded and
chopped**

2 **to 3 large** garlic cloves

3 **tablespoons** chili powder,
preferably Gerhardt's brand

1 **tablespoon** sweet smoked paprika

1 **tablespoon ground** cumin,
a palmful

1 **tablespoon ground** coriander,
a palmful

½ **cup** tomato paste

2 **to 3 cups turkey or** chicken stock

2 **cups shredded** sharp yellow
cheddar cheese

lemon risotto

1 quart chicken stock

1 tablespoon EVOO (extra-virgin olive oil)

1 small to medium onion, finely chopped

2 garlic cloves, finely chopped or grated

1 cup arborio rice

Zest and juice of 1 large lemon or 2 small Meyer lemons

½ cup dry white wine

Salt and black pepper

2 tablespoons butter, cut into small pieces

½ cup grated Pecorino Romano cheese, a couple handfuls

2 tablespoons slivered fresh mint leaves

A handful of basil leaves, shredded or torn

In a medium saucepan, heat the stock and 2 cups of water over medium-low heat. ■ In a risotto pot or large skillet with a rounded bottom, heat the EVOO over medium to medium-high heat. Add the onions and garlic to the risotto pot and sauté to soften for 3 to 4 minutes. Stir in the rice and add the zest of the lemon, then heat the rice for 1 to 2 minutes before adding the wine and cooking to evaporate. A few ladles at a time, add the warm stock and stir for a minute each time to develop the starch (this will make the risotto creamy). Keep adding stock each time the pan starts to become dry at the edges. The total cooking time will be 18 minutes or so. When the rice is cooked to al dente, season with salt and pepper, and stir in the butter, lemon juice, cheese, and herbs. Garnish with lemon zest and herbs. Serve immediately.

orange balsamic
glazed chicken

In a large skillet, heat the EVOO over medium-high to high heat. ■ Season the chicken liberally with salt, pepper, and poultry seasoning. Add the chicken to the pan when the oil ripples and brown for 5 minutes. Turn the chicken and season with the rosemary. Cook for 5 minutes more. ■ Stir together the marmalade, vinegar, and stock and pour over the chicken. Let sauce thicken slightly, 2 to 3 minutes, until it reaches a thin glaze consistency. Add the scallions during the last minute of cooking time. Slice the chicken and serve the pieces topped with the arugula.

2 tablespoons EVOO (extra-virgin olive oil)

2 pounds boneless skinless chicken, **thighs or breasts or a combination of light and dark meat**

Salt **and coarse** black pepper

1 teaspoon poultry seasoning

2 to 3 sprigs of fresh rosemary, **leaves removed and chopped**

⅓ cup orange marmalade

¼ cup balsamic vinegar

½ cup chicken stock

2 scallions, **white and green parts, finely chopped**

4 cups baby arugula

This is a **double recipe in one**: Serve either as a stand-alone entrée OR serve the sliced chicken and greens in a delightful puddle of creamy lemon risotto for a meal that will surely impress.

This meal is full of flavor. It reminds me of a lunch I had with John in Italy. Try adding **Bruschetta with Hot Cherry Tomatoes** (page 267).

fettuccine with
garden vegetables & greens

Heat a large pot of water to boil for the pasta. When boiling, salt the water and cook the pasta to just shy of al dente. ■ Meanwhile, heat 2 tablespoons of the EVOO in a large skillet over medium heat. Add the onions, garlic, eggplant, zucchini, and bell pepper as you chop them. Season the vegetables with salt and cover. Cook for 10 to 12 minutes until tender. ■ Just before draining the pasta, add about 1 cup of starchy cooking liquid to the vegetables, then drain the pasta and add it to the vegetables. Toss to combine, then add the basil and cheese and a little black pepper to taste. Top the pasta with the shredded lettuce, sprinkle with extra cheese, and drizzle with the remaining tablespoon of EVOO.

SERVES 4

Salt

1 pound fettuccine

3 tablespoons EVOO (extra-virgin olive oil)

1 small onion, very thinly sliced

2 garlic cloves, chopped or sliced

2 to 3 small firm eggplant, about 1 pound, peeled and julienned (Japanese eggplant may be substituted)

2 medium zucchini, sliced into julienne or matchsticks

1 small red bell pepper, seeded, rounded ends trimmed, and thinly sliced

A generous handful of fresh basil leaves, shredded

½ cup grated Pecorino Romano cheese, plus more for garnish

Black pepper

8 to 10 leaves green or red leaf lettuce, shredded

glazed chicken & peaches
with cheese & bacon biscuits

SERVES 4

1 tablespoon **EVOO** (extra-virgin olive oil), **plus some for drizzling**

2 slices smoky bacon, **finely chopped**

1 box of biscuit mix, such as Jiffy, or **mix for 8 drop biscuits**

⅛ teaspoon freshly grated nutmeg

1 cup shredded sharp yellow cheddar cheese

2 tablespoons butter

4 peaches, **halved or thickly sliced**

½ lemon

2 boneless skinless chicken breast **halves**

4 boneless skinless chicken thighs

Salt **and** pepper

1 shallot, **chopped**

2 inches of fresh gingerroot, **peeled and grated or minced**

¾ **cup** chicken stock

⅔ **cup** peach preserves

2 teaspoons hot sauce

2 tablespoons Worcestershire sauce

2 tablespoons fresh thyme leaves, **chopped**

Preheat the oven to the temperature called for in the package directions for the biscuits. ■ Heat a small skillet over medium-high heat with a drizzle of EVOO, about ½ teaspoon. Add the bacon and cook for 2 to 3 minutes until crisp. ■ Place the biscuit mix in a bowl and add the nutmeg. Continue to follow the package directions, then mix in the bacon, 1 tablespoon drippings, and form the biscuit dough. Then fold in half of the cheese, arrange the drop biscuits on a baking sheet, and top with a sprinkle of cheese. Bake for 10 to 12 minutes, until golden. Remove from the oven to cool. ■ While the biscuits bake, prepare the peaches and the chicken. Heat a skillet with the butter over medium heat. Add the peaches and the juice of the lemon half, then cook for 10 minutes or until tender and lightly golden. Turn off the heat. ■ While the peaches cook, heat 1 tablespoon of the EVOO in a large nonstick skillet over medium-high to high heat. Cut the chicken breast pieces in half across the center of each breast to make 4 equal portions. Add the chicken breasts and thighs to the pan and season with salt and pepper. Cook for 12 minutes, turn halfway through, transfer to a plate, and cover with foil. Add another drizzle of EVOO to the pan. Add the shallot and ginger, then add the stock, peach preserves, hot sauce, and Worcestershire sauce. Season with pepper and cook for a couple of minutes over medium heat until the glaze is thickened. Arrange the chicken and peaches on a platter, douse with the glaze, and garnish with the thyme. Serve 1 piece of breast meat and 1 thigh per person. Pass the biscuits at the table.

To add a fancy but easy extra course, pair with **Sweet Onion Potatoes Au Gratin** (page 268).

Serve with wilted spinach or try the **Spinach, Mushroom, and Balsamic-Cream Crostini** (page 269).

chicken ragù

Heat a large pot of water to a boil for the pasta. Salt the water when it boils and cook the pasta to al dente. ■ In a large skillet, heat 2 tablespoons of the EVOO over medium-high heat. Brown the pancetta for 3 to 4 minutes, then add another tablespoon of EVOO. Add the chicken and brown evenly for 5 to 6 minutes. Add the onions, rosemary, and garlic, then season with salt and pepper. Grate the carrot with a box grater directly into the pan and stir in. Add the bay leaf and cook until the vegetables are soft, 5 to 6 minutes. ■ Add the wine to the chicken and vegetables, stir and reduce for a minute, then add the tomatoes and crush them with a wooden spoon. Simmer for a few minutes to thicken the sauce and combine the flavors. ■ Drain the pasta and toss with the chicken ragù and cheese. Discard the bay leaf. Garnish with some torn basil. Serve immediately.

SERVES 4

Salt

1 pound whole-wheat or whole-grain rigatoni or other short cut pasta

3 tablespoons EVOO (extra-virgin olive oil)

¼ pound pancetta, **a couple thick slices, cut into fine dice**

1½ pounds chicken thighs, **chopped into small bite-size pieces**

1 medium to large onion, **chopped**

2 to 3 sprigs of fresh rosemary, **leaves stripped and finely chopped**

2 to 3 garlic cloves, **finely chopped**

Black pepper

1 carrot, **peeled**

1 bay leaf

½ cup Marsala, **a couple glugs**

1 (28-ounce) can San Marzano tomatoes

Grated Parmigiano-Reggiano **cheese**

A handful of fresh basil leaves, **torn**

sausage & fish one-pot

SERVES 4

1 tablespoon **EVOO** (extra-virgin olive oil), plus some for liberal drizzling to garnish

½ **pound bulk** Italian hot sausage

2 **large** garlic cloves

1 **medium** onion

1½ **pounds baby red or Yukon Gold** potatoes

Salt **and** pepper

½ **cup** dry vermouth **or dry white wine**

1 **pint** cherry tomatoes, **halved**

4 haddock **or cod fillets**

A handful of fresh flat-leaf parsley, chopped

½ lemon

Crusty bread, to pass at the table

In a skillet with a tight-fitting lid, heat the tablespoon of EVOO over medium-high heat. Brown the sausage for 3 to 4 minutes, breaking it down into crumbles as it cooks. While the sausage browns, crush the garlic and trim off the root ends, then thinly slice the onion and potatoes. ■ Add the garlic, onions, and potatoes to the pan and toss to combine with the sausage. Season with salt and pepper. ■ Douse the pan with half the vermouth or wine, set the lid in place, and cook for 10 to 12 minutes. ■ Add the tomatoes to the pan and gently fold into the mixture. Set the fillets atop the mixture and douse with the remaining vermouth or wine. ■ Season the fish with salt and pepper. Set the lid in place and cook for 6 to 8 minutes, until the fish is opaque. ■ Top the cooked fish with the parsley, sprinkle with the juice of the lemon half, and drizzle liberally with EVOO. ■ Serve the mixture at the table from the pan into shallow bowls to hold the juice. ■ Soak crusty bread in the pan drippings and pass at the table.

This meal is **so easy** that you may be up for a dessert. **Try the Limoncello and Lemon Cream Fruit Tart** (page 303).

sausage & onion kebabs
on roasted pepper salad

These skewers can be prepared on the outdoor grill or under the broiler. If cooking on the grill, preheat to medium-high. ■ Heat the broiler to high. Place the peppers on a rimmed baking sheet and broil for about 15 minutes, turning to char them evenly. Leave the door cracked open a bit so steam can escape. ■ While the peppers roast and blacken, bring a couple inches of water to boil in a skillet. Add the sausages and par-cook them through for 7 to 8 minutes. ■ While the sausages cook, bring a medium-size pot of water to a boil. Add the cipollini onions and cook for 5 minutes. Remove the sausages and drain the boiling onions, then wipe off the skins and trim off the ends with a paring knife. ■ Cut each sausage into 3 pieces. On each of 8 metal skewers, thread 3 pieces of sausage and 3 onions. Drizzle the skewers with EVOO, season with salt and pepper, and reserve. ■ Place the roasted peppers in a bowl and cover tightly with plastic wrap. If using the broiler for the kebabs, leave it on but drop the rack a few inches. If you are grilling outside, switch the broiler off. ■ Cool the peppers for 10 minutes so you can handle them. Peel and seed them, then chop into 2-inch squares or slice into 2-inch-wide strips. Dress with a liberal drizzle of EVOO, season with salt and pepper, and sprinkle the chopped red onion and hot pepper rings on top. ■ In a 6-inch skillet over low heat, or on the side of the outside grill, melt the butter, stir in the garlic and parsley, and reserve. ■ Grill or broil the skewers for 5 to 6 minutes, turning every couple of minutes. Baste with the vinegar in the last minute of cooking time. ■ Char the bread on the grill for the last 2 minutes of cooking time and dip it in the garlic-parsley butter. ■ On a serving platter, arrange the sausage and onions on a bed of dressed peppers and surround with chunks of garlic toast. Remove the metal skewers and serve.

SERVES 4

2 **large** red bell peppers

2 **large** green bell peppers

2 **large** yellow bell peppers

8 **fresh** Italian pork or chicken sausage links

24 cipollini onions

EVOO (extra-virgin olive oil) for liberal drizzling

Salt **and** pepper

¼ red onion, **finely chopped**

3 to 4 tablespoons hot pepper rings, **finely chopped**

6 tablespoons (¾ stick) butter

4 garlic cloves, **finely chopped**

1 small bunch of fresh flat-leaf parsley, **chopped**

Aged balsamic vinegar, **for basting**

1 loaf ciabatta bread, **split and cut into 8 pieces**

yellow chicken & rice

SERVES 4

1 **quart** chicken stock

½ **teaspoon (about 2 pinches)** saffron threads

1 **tablespoon** EVOO **(extra-virgin olive oil)**

3 **tablespoons** butter, **divided**

8 **bone-in skin-on** chicken thighs **or 4 bone-in skin-on chicken breasts, cut in half**

Salt **and** pepper

⅓ **to ½ cup (a couple of handfuls) broken** spaghetti

1 **cup** long-grain rice

1 **medium** onion, **chopped**

2 garlic cloves, **finely chopped or grated**

1 **bay leaf**

1 **pinch of ground** cinnamon

1 **pinch of ground** turmeric

¼ **cup chopped fresh** flat-leaf parsley

1 **cup** frozen peas

Place a medium-size pot over medium heat with the chicken stock and saffron. Bring them up to a simmer and keep warm. ■ Place a large, high-sided skillet over medium-high heat with the EVOO and 1 tablespoon of the butter. Season the chicken with salt and pepper, and cook in the pan until golden brown, 4 to 5 minutes per side. Remove the chicken to a plate and reserve, covered with foil. ■ Melt the remaining 2 tablespoons butter in the pan. Add the pasta to the pan and cook until toasted and golden brown, 2 to 3 minutes. Remove the foil from the chicken and add the rice to the pan, tossing to coat in the butter, along with the onion and garlic. Cook, stirring occasionally, until the veggies are tender, about 5 minutes. ■ Add the bay leaf, cinnamon, turmeric, reserved chicken, and saffron-infused stock to the pan. Bring the liquid up to a bubble, cover the pan, then reduce the heat to medium and simmer until the chicken is cooked through and the rice is tender, 15 to 18 minutes. Stir in the parsley and peas, discard the bay leaf, and serve.

My buddy Bobby Flay **LOVES** ancho chiles and describes them as spicy raisins. You're gonna love this soup's flavor.

This is a very filling supper, but if a few friends are sharing, try the **Chorizo Mushroom Queso Dip** (page 273).

ancho chicken
tortilla soup

Preheat the oven to 350°F. Slice the tortillas into ½-inch-wide strips and scatter on a large rimmed baking sheet. Spray with cooking spray and bake until golden and crisp. Remove the tortilla chips and reserve. ■ While the tortillas crisp, in a medium saucepan heat the anchos with the stock. Bring to a boil, then reduce the heat to low and simmer until the anchos are tender, about 15 minutes. ■ While the anchos simmer, heat a medium soup pot with the vegetable oil over high heat. Add the corn and char at the edges for 2 to 3 minutes. Reduce the heat a little and add the onions, peppers, and garlic. Season with the cumin, smoked paprika, and cinnamon, sauté for 5 minutes, then add the beer. Cook for 1 minute, then stir in the tomatoes. ■ Puree the anchos and stock in a food processor, then add to the soup pot. Stir in the honey, then add the shredded chicken, salt, and pepper. Thin the soup with 1 cup of water (2 cups for thinner soup) and simmer to combine the flavors. ■ Add the zest and juice of 1 lime to the soup. Seed and dice the avocados and dress them with the juice of the second lime. ■ Pile up the tortilla strips in a soup bowl. Top the strips with diced avocado, ladle the soup over the top, and garnish with sour cream, whole or chopped cilantro leaves, and more tortilla strips.

6 (6-inch) flour tortillas

Cooking spray

2 large ancho chiles, **seeded and stemmed**

1 quart chicken stock

2 tablespoons vegetable oil

2 ears corn on the cob, **shucked, kernels scraped from the cob, or 1 cup frozen kernels, defrosted**

1 large red onion, **chopped**

1 jalapeño pepper, **seeded and chopped or thinly sliced**

1 red chile pepper, **seeded and chopped or thinly sliced**

2 garlic cloves, **finely chopped**

1 teaspoon ground cumin, **⅓ palmful**

1½ teaspoons sweet smoked paprika, **½ palmful**

½ teaspoon ground cinnamon **(eyeball it in your palm)**

1 bottle Mexican beer, **such as Dos Equis**

1 (28-ounce) can diced or crushed fire-roasted tomatoes

1 tablespoon honey

1 rotisserie chicken, **skinned and shredded**

Salt **and** pepper

2 limes

2 ripe Hass avocados

Sour cream

Cilantro leaves, **for garnish**

three-bean
pasta e fagioli

Heat the EVOO in a soup pot over medium to medium-high heat. Add the celery, onions, carrot, garlic, rosemary, bay leaf, salt, and pepper and sauté for 7 to 8 minutes to soften the vegetables. Stir in the tomato paste, cannellini beans, and chickpeas for 1 minute. Add the stock and 3 cups water, cover, and bring to a boil. Add the pasta and simmer in the soup for 5 minutes, then add the green beans and simmer together for 3 to 4 more minutes, until the pasta is al dente and the beans are cooked through. Turn off the heat and add the juice and zest of the lemon and the parsley; adjust the salt and pepper. Discard the bay leaf. Serve in shallow bowls and sprinkle cheese on top.

SERVES 4

2 tablespoons EVOO **(extra-virgin olive oil)**

3 to 4 celery stalks, **from the heart, chopped**

1 medium onion, **chopped**

1 carrot, **peeled and chopped**

2 garlic cloves, **finely chopped**

2 stems fresh rosemary

1 bay leaf, **fresh or dried**

Salt **and** pepper

3 tablespoons tomato paste

1 (15-ounce) can cannellini beans

1 (15-ounce) can chickpeas

3 cups chicken stock

1 cup mini penne rigate **(with ridges) or ditalini**

¼ pound fresh green beans, **trimmed and cut into thirds on an angle**

Zest and juice of 1 lemon

A handful of fresh flat-leaf parsley, **finely chopped**

Grated Pecorino Romano **cheese, for topping**

paprika chicken with egg noodles

Bring a large pot of water to a boil, salt the water, and cook the noodles to al dente. ■ While the water is coming to a boil, place a large skillet over medium-high heat with the EVOO. Season the chicken liberally with salt and pepper and brown the meat for a few minutes on each side. Transfer to a plate and reserve. ■ Add the garlic, bell peppers, and onions to the pan, season with salt and pepper, and cook to soften, 7 to 8 minutes. Add a drizzle more EVOO if the pan seems dry. Add the chicken back to the pan and stir in the paprika, allspice, and stock. When the stock comes to a bubble, reduce the heat to a simmer and cook for 5 more minutes. Turn off the heat and stir in the sour cream. ■ Drain the egg noodles and return them to the hot pot. Toss with the butter, dill, and chives to coat. ■ Ladle the chicken over the noodles in shallow bowls and top with chopped cornichons or gherkin pickles.

Salt

½ pound extra-wide egg noodles

2 tablespoons EVOO (extra-virgin olive oil), **plus more if needed**

2 pounds boneless skinless chicken, **dark or white meat, cut into 1-inch pieces**

Black pepper

2 garlic cloves, **finely chopped**

2 red bell peppers, **seeded, quartered lengthwise, and thinly sliced**

1 large onion, **quartered lengthwise then thinly sliced**

2 round tablespoons ground sweet paprika, **a couple palmfuls**

½ teaspoon ground allspice **(eyeball it in your palm)**

2 cups chicken stock

1 cup sour cream

2 tablespoons butter, **cut into small pieces**

2 to 3 tablespoons finely chopped fresh dill

2 to 3 tablespoons finely chopped fresh chives

¼ cup chopped cornichons **or baby gherkin pickles**

spinach & artichoke
mac 'n' cheese

Bring a large pot of water to a boil for the pasta, salt the water, and cook the pasta to al dente. ■ While the pasta water comes to a boil, place a medium pot over medium-low heat with EVOO and the butter. Add the onions and garlic to the pan and cook until very soft, about 10 minutes. ■ Heat the broiler and position the rack in the middle of the oven. ■ Turn up the heat under the pot to medium-high and sprinkle the flour into the pot. Cook for about 1 minute, then whisk in the wine and cook for another minute to burn off the alcohol. Whisk the milk into the pan and bring up to a bubble. Add the nutmeg, artichokes, spinach, and salt and pepper to the sauce and simmer until thickened and the vegetables are warmed through, 2 to 3 minutes more. Add 1 cup of each of the cheeses to the sauce and stir until melted. ■ Toss the prepared sauce with the cooked pasta and transfer to a casserole dish. Sprinkle the remaining Fontina and Parmigiano over the top and brown under the broiler for about 3 minutes.

SERVES 4

Salt

1 pound semolina or whole-wheat penne

2 tablespoons EVOO (extra-virgin olive oil)

3 tablespoons butter

1 medium onion, **finely chopped**

3 garlic cloves, **finely chopped or grated**

3 tablespoons all-purpose flour

½ cup dry white wine

2 cups whole milk

¼ teaspoon freshly grated nutmeg, **or to taste**

1 (10-ounce) box frozen chopped artichokes, **defrosted and drained**

1 (10-ounce) box frozen chopped spinach, **defrosted and wrung dry in a kitchen towel**

Black pepper

1½ cups shredded Italian Fontina cheese, **plus additional for sprinkling on top**

1½ cups grated Parmigiano-Reggiano cheese, **plus additional for sprinkling on top**

bolognese with
pappardelle

In a large pot, heat the EVOO over medium-high heat, then add the pancetta and cook, stirring occasionally, until it is browned and the fat is rendered, 3 to 4 minutes. Add the sirloin and pork to the pot and brown for 8 to 10 minutes, stirring occasionally to break up the lumps. Add the onions, garlic, carrot, and celery and cook, stirring, until the vegetables are softened, 6 to 7 minutes. ■ Add salt and pepper and the nutmeg, bay leaves, thyme, marjoram or oregano, and red pepper flakes. Add the tomato paste and stir for a minute or so, then add the wine and scrape up all the drippings. Reduce the wine by half for 2 to 3 minutes, then stir in the stock and bring to a boil. Reduce the heat to a simmer and thicken the sauce for 1 to 1½ hours, stirring occasionally to keep the sauce from sticking to the bottom of the pot. ■ When you're ready to serve, bring a large pot of water to a boil, salt the water, and cook the pasta to al dente. ■ Add the milk to the sauce and simmer for a couple minutes to heat through. Discard the bay leaves and adjust the seasonings to taste. Turn off the heat. ■ Once the pasta is done, reserve about a cup of pasta water before draining. Drain the pasta and toss it back into the pot it was cooked in along with the reserved water, about a cup of grated cheese, and a couple handfuls of chopped parsley. Add half the pasta sauce and toss well to coat. ■ Serve the pasta in shallow bowls, topped with additional sauce. Pass the remaining cheese at the table.

SERVES 4 TO 6

2 tablespoons EVOO (extra-virgin olive oil)

¼ pound pancetta, cut into small dice or ground

1 pound ground sirloin

1 pound ground pork

1 onion, cut into small dice

3 to 4 garlic cloves, minced or grated

1 carrot, cut into small dice

2 celery stalks, cut into small dice

Salt and pepper

¼ teaspoon freshy grated nutmeg, or to taste

2 bay leaves

1 tablespoon fresh thyme leaves, a couple of sprigs, chopped

1 teaspoon dried marjoram or oregano, ⅓ palmful

½ teaspoon crushed red pepper flakes

¼ cup tomato paste

2 cups red wine

3 cups beef stock

1 pound pappardelle or fettuccine pasta

1 cup whole milk or half-and-half

1 cup grated Parmigiano-Reggiano cheese, plus more to pass at the table

½ cup chopped fresh flat-leaf parsley, a couple handfuls

midwinter minestrone

SERVES 4

2 tablespoons EVOO (extra-virgin olive oil)

¼ pound sliced pancetta, cut into ¼-inch dice (optional)

2 carrots, peeled and chopped into ¼-inch dice

3 celery stalks, chopped into ¼-inch dice

2 bay leaves, fresh or dried

3 to 4 garlic cloves, finely chopped or grated

1 large or 2 medium red onions, chopped

Salt and pepper

1 ounce dried porcini or mixed wild mushrooms, chopped

½ cup soft sun-dried tomatoes, thinly sliced

1 quart chicken or vegetable stock

1 small bunch of purple or green kale, washed and dried

1 cup semolina or whole-wheat ditalini or other short cut pasta

1 (15-ounce) can chickpeas

Pecorino Romano cheese, grated or shredded, to pass at the table

Place a heavy-bottomed soup pot over medium-high heat with the EVOO. Add the pancetta to the pot (if using) and cook until crispy, 3 to 4 minutes. Add the carrots, celery, bay leaves, garlic, and onions to the pot, season with salt and pepper, and cook until the veggies are tender, 7 to 8 minutes more. ■ Add the mushrooms, sun-dried tomatoes, stock, and 2 cups water to the pot, and bring up to a boil. ■ Hold the kale by the stems and curl up your opposite hand around the greens at the base of the stem. With a quick jerking motion strip the greens off and away from the stems and chop the greens. ■ Add the kale, pasta, and chickpeas to the soup pot, and cook until the pasta is al dente. Season the soup with salt and pepper to taste. Discard the bay leaves. ■ Ladle the soup into shallow bowls, top with the Pecorino Romano, and serve.

Most Creole and Cajun recipes start with the "holy trinity" of onion, celery, and bell peppers. I've combined these flavors to make a killer Trinity Gravy.

creole meat loaves with
trinity gravy & buttermilk sweet potatoes

Cover the potatoes with water in a medium pot and bring to a boil, then season with salt and cook for 12 to 15 minutes until tender. When the potatoes are ready, drain and return them to the hot pot and mash with the buttermilk to the desired consistency. ■ Preheat the oven to 375°F. ■ Heat the tablespoon of EVOO in a medium skillet over medium heat, add one quarter of the onions and half of the garlic to the skillet, and cook to soften, 5 to 6 minutes. Transfer the mixture to a bowl and cool. To the cooled onion mixture add the pork, paprika, thyme, salt and pepper to taste, mustard, bread crumbs, and egg. Mix to combine and form four 2-inch-thick loaves. Arrange on a parchment-lined rimmed baking sheet and drizzle liberally with EVOO, then roast for 35 to 40 minutes until firm and golden. ■ To the same skillet add the butter and when it has melted, add the remaining onions and garlic, the celery, bell pepper, and salt and pepper to taste. Cook to soften, 5 to 6 minutes. Add the tomato paste and stir for 1 minute. Sprinkle the flour over the mixture and stir for another minute. Stir in the stock, then the hot sauce, and cook to thicken over medium-low heat for a couple of minutes. Turn the heat to the lowest setting to keep the gravy warm. ■ Slice the meat loaves. Arrange the sliced loaves alongside the buttermilk potatoes and pour the trinity gravy over both. Garnish with the scallions and serve.

SERVES 4

2 pounds sweet potatoes**, peeled and cut into chunks**

Salt

¾ to 1 cup buttermilk

1 tablespoon EVOO **(extra-virgin olive oil), plus more for drizzling**

1 large red or yellow onion**, finely chopped**

4 garlic cloves**, finely chopped**

2 pounds ground pork

1 tablespoon sweet paprika

2 tablespoons fresh thyme leaves**, chopped**

Black pepper

¼ cup grainy mustard

½ cup bread crumbs**, a couple handfuls**

1 egg

2 tablespoons butter

2 celery stalks**, chopped**

1 green bell pepper**, seeded and chopped**

2 tablespoons tomato paste

2 tablespoons all-purpose flour

1½ cups chicken stock

2 to 3 tablespoons hot sauce**, depending on how spicy you like it**

4 to 5 scallions**, sliced on the bias, for garnish**

fajita chilaquiles casserole

SERVES 4

8 (6-inch) flour tortillas, **cut into 1-inch-wide strips**

Cooking spray

1 tablespoon onion powder, **a palmful**

1 tablespoon garlic powder, **a palmful**

1 tablespoon ground cumin, **a palmful**

1 teaspoon ground cinnamon, **⅓ palmful**

1 tablespoon chili powder, **a palmful**

1 teaspoon dried oregano, **⅓ palmful**

1½ pounds sirloin steak or boneless skinless chicken breasts **or boneless pork chops, thinly sliced**

Salt **and** pepper

4 tablespoons high-temp cooking oil, such as safflower or peanut or vegetable

1 bottle Mexican beer

2 red bell peppers, **seeded and thinly sliced**

2 red onions, **thinly sliced**

3 to 4 garlic cloves, **finely chopped or grated**

¼ cup chopped fresh cilantro **or flat-leaf parsley leaves**

2 limes

2 cups shredded pepper Jack cheese

Sour cream, **for garnish**

Salsa, **store-bought or homemade**

Preheat the oven to 400°F. ■ On a rimmed baking sheet, arrange the tortilla strips in a single layer and spray with cooking spray to coat. Bake until crispy, 7 to 8 minutes. When you remove the tortilla strips, turn on the broiler and place a rack in the middle of the oven. ■ In a small bowl, combine the onion powder, garlic powder, cumin, cinnamon, chili powder, and oregano. Season the meat with salt and pepper, then toss with the spice rub to coat evenly. ■ Place a large skillet over high heat with 2 tablespoons of the oil. Add the meat to the pan and sear, caramelizing the meat a few minutes on each side. Add the beer to the pan and cook to reduce, 2 minutes. ■ While the meat is cooking, place a second large skillet over high heat with the remaining 2 tablespoons of oil. Add the bell peppers, onions, and garlic to the pan, and cook until the vegetables are brown around the edges and tender, 3 to 4 minutes. Add the chopped cilantro or parsley, the juice of 1 lime, and salt and pepper, and toss to combine. Remove from the heat. ■ Combine the meat, peppers and onions, and toasted tortilla strips together into a casserole dish. Top with the cheese and place under the broiler to melt the cheese, about 3 minutes. Garnish with the juice of the remaining lime, sour cream, and salsa.

hungarian-style chili
with polenta

Heat a large pot over medium-high to high heat with the EVOO. Add the beef and brown for 7 to 8 minutes, stirring occasionally to break up the lumps. Add the chile pepper, bell pepper, onions, and garlic and season with salt and pepper. Cook 7 to 8 more minutes to soften the vegetables. Stir in the chili powder, sweet paprika, and marjoram. Add the tomato paste to the pot and stir to combine, 1 minute. Add the beef stock to the pot and bring the chili to a boil. Reduce the heat to a simmer and cook for 15 minutes. ■ In a medium saucepan, bring the water or chicken stock and the milk to a boil, whisk in the polenta, and cook for 2 to 3 minutes until thickened. Stir in the cheese and butter and season with salt and pepper. ■ Fill shallow bowls with polenta, making a well in the center. Fill the well with ladles of chili and top with sour cream, dill, parsley, and chives.

SERVES 4

2 tablespoons **EVOO (extra-virgin olive oil)**

2 pounds coarse-ground sirloin

1 red chile pepper, **seeded and finely chopped**

1 red bell pepper, **seeded and chopped**

1 large onion, **chopped**

4 garlic cloves, **finely chopped**

Salt **and** pepper

1½ tablespoons chili powder, **1½ palmfuls**

1½ tablespoons sweet smoked paprika, **1½ palmfuls**

1 teaspoon dried marjoram **or oregano, ⅓ palmful**

¼ cup tomato paste

1 quart beef stock

1½ cups water or chicken stock

1½ cups milk

1 cup quick-cooking polenta

1 cup shredded Gouda **or smoked Gouda cheese**

2 tablespoons butter

1 cup sour cream

Chopped fresh dill, flat-leaf parsley, **and** chives, **for garnish**

shepherd's pie
stuffed potatoes

Preheat the oven to 400°F. ■ On a rimmed baking sheet, toss the potatoes with a hearty drizzle of EVOO and some salt. Bake until tender, about 1 hour, then let cool. Turn off the oven and switch on the broiler. ■ While the potatoes cool, heat 1 tablespoon of the EVOO in a medium skillet over medium heat. Add the bell pepper and half of the onions and sauté to soften for 5 minutes, then set aside to cool. ■ When the potatoes are cool enough to handle, cut a thin top slice off each potato. In a mixing bowl add the bell pepper and onion mixture, the sour cream, smoked paprika, half of the Gouda, salt, and pepper. Scoop in the potato flesh and mash to combine. Reserve. ■ Meanwhile, place a large skillet over medium-high heat with the remaining 2 tablespoons of EVOO. Add the ground sirloin to the pan and brown for 5 to 6 minutes, stirring occasionally to break up the lumps. Add the mushrooms and cook until they start to turn golden brown, 4 to 5 minutes more. Add the remaining onions and the garlic and cook for another 5 minutes. Push all of the ingredients to the edges of the pan and add the butter to the middle of the skillet. Sprinkle the flour over the melted butter and cook for about 1 minute. Whisk in the stock, mustard, soy sauce, and Worcestershire. Bring up to a bubble, combine with the meat mixture, adjust the salt and pepper, and simmer until thickened, 2 to 3 minutes. ■ Fill the potato shells with the beef and veggie mixture, then top each of them with the reserved mashed potatoes. Transfer to a baking sheet and sprinkle with the remaining cheese. Pop the potatoes under the broiler until the cheese is melted and the tops are golden brown, a minute or two.

SERVES 4

4 large russet potatoes, **scrubbed clean**

3 tablespoons EVOO (extra-virgin olive oil), **plus more for drizzling**

Salt

½ red bell pepper, **seeded and chopped**

1 medium onion, **chopped**

½ cup sour cream

1 tablespoon smoked paprika

1 cup shredded smoked Gouda cheese

Black pepper

1 pound ground sirloin

½ pound button or cremini mushrooms, **quartered**

2 garlic cloves, **finely chopped or grated**

2 tablespoons butter

2 tablespoons all-purpose flour

1½ cups beef stock

2 tablespoons spicy brown or Dijon mustard

2 tablespoons soy sauce

2 tablespoons Worcestershire sauce

chipotle chicken chili with
flaming tequila-pepper salsa & avocado ranch dressing

SERVES 4

4 tablespoons EVOO (extra-virgin olive oil)

6 slices smoky bacon, **chopped**

2 pounds ground chicken breast

2 to 3 tablespoons pureed chipotle in adobo, **depending on preferred heat level**

1 tablespoon ground cumin

1 tablespoon ground coriander

1 tablespoon smoked paprika

1 large yellow onion, **chopped**

3 to 4 garlic cloves, **finely chopped or grated**

3 tablespoons tomato paste

1 quart chicken stock

Salt **and** pepper

1 yellow bell pepper, **seeded and chopped**

1 red bell pepper, **seeded and chopped**

1 orange bell pepper, **seeded and chopped**

1 medium red onion, **chopped**

2 jalapeño peppers, **seeded and finely chopped**

4 shots of tequila

Juice of 1 lime

¼ cup chopped fresh cilantro leaves

1 avocado, **pitted**

¼ cup finely chopped fresh chives

Juice of 1 lemon

1 cup buttermilk

Crushed tortilla chips, **for garnish**

Place a large heavy-bottomed pot over medium-high heat with 2 tablespoons of the EVOO. Add the bacon to the pan and brown, about 3 to 4 minutes. Add the chicken to the pot and brown, 5 to 6 minutes, stirring occasionally to break up the lumps. Add the pureed chipotle, cumin, coriander, and smoked paprika, then stir for 1 minute. Add the onion and garlic to the pot and cook until tender, 5 minutes more. Add the tomato paste and chicken stock and some salt and pepper to the pot and bring the liquids up to a bubble. Reduce the heat to a simmer. ■ While the chili is simmering, place a medium skillet over medium-high heat with the remaining 2 tablespoons of EVOO. Add the bell peppers, red onion, and jalapeño to the skillet and cook until tender, 4 to 5 minutes. Remove the skillet from the heat and add the tequila. Return the skillet to the heat and flame the tequila to burn off most of the alcohol. Add the lime juice, the cilantro, and some salt to the salsa. ■ To a food processor bowl add the avocado, chives, lemon juice, and buttermilk. Process until smooth and then season with salt and pepper. ■ Serve up the chili with some of the tequila-pepper salsa and avocado ranch dressing. Garnish with tortilla chips.

Bring home **a bushel of corn** at summer's end, cook the ears, and scrape and freeze the kernels for **year-round enjoyment**.

summer corn fettuccine

Heat a large pot of water to boil for the pasta. Salt the water and cook the pasta to al dente. ■ Meanwhile, heat a large skillet with a drizzle of EVOO over medium to medium-high heat. Add the bacon to the pan and cook for a few minutes to crisp the bacon and render its fat. Place a small bowl inverted in a large bowl, steady the corn cobs on the smaller bowl, and scrape the kernels off the ears. Add three quarters of the kernels and liquids to the bacon. Add the shallots and bell pepper to the corn mixture and season liberally with salt and pepper. Cook until tender, 5 to 6 minutes. ■ Add the remaining corn to the food processor and puree with the cream. ■ Stir in the thyme and the stock or wine into the corn mixture in the skillet, reduce for a minute, then stir in the corn-cream mixture. Reduce the heat to a simmer. Cook for 3 to 4 minutes, stirring frequently, to thicken. Add the hot sauce or cayenne pepper and adjust the salt and pepper. ■ Drain the pasta, then toss with the sauce, parsley, and a couple handfuls of cheese, about ½ cup. Top with the basil or tarragon and pass the remaining cheese at the table.

SERVES 4 TO 6

Salt

1 pound fettuccine

EVOO (extra virgin olive oil), for drizzling

6 slices smoky bacon, chopped

6 ears corn on the cob, shucked

3 shallots, finely chopped

1 small red bell pepper, seeded and chopped

Black pepper

1 cup half-and-half or cream—whatever you put in your morning coffee

2 tablespoons fresh thyme leaves

½ cup chicken stock or dry white wine

A few dashes of hot sauce or a pinch or two of cayenne pepper

A couple handfuls of chopped fresh flat-leaf parsley

1 cup grated Parmigiano-Reggiano cheese

½ cup chopped fresh sweet basil leaves or ¼ cup chopped fresh tarragon leaves

spanish-style chicken & dumplings

In a small sauce pot, combine the stock and saffron, bring to a bubble, then reduce the heat and simmer over low heat to allow the saffron to steep. ■ In a large deep skillet with a lid or a Dutch oven, heat the EVOO over medium-high heat. Add the chorizo, cook for 2 minutes to render some of the fat, then add the chicken and lightly brown. Add the onions, thyme, garlic, bay leaf, salt and pepper, and the mushrooms, softening the vegetables for 5 minutes. Sprinkle in the flour, stir, add the sherry, and stir for a minute more. Then throw in the peas and add the saffron broth to the pan. ■ While the vegetables soften, place the biscuit mix in a bowl and stir in the parsley and paprika. Remove the bay leaf, then add the liquids, following the package directions. ■ Drop 8 small mounds of biscuit dough onto the surface of the chicken and sauce, cover with a tight-fitting lid, and cook for 8 to 10 minutes. ■ Serve in shallow bowls.

1 quart chicken stock

2 pinches of saffron

2 tablespoons EVOO (extra-virgin olive oil)

¾ pound chorizo, casing removed, chopped or crumbled

1 pound boneless skinless chicken thighs or breast tenders, diced

1 medium onion, chopped

2 tablespoons fresh thyme leaves

2 to 3 large garlic cloves, chopped

1 bay leaf, fresh or dried

Salt and pepper

¾ pound medium to large white mushrooms, quartered

2 rounded tablespoons all-purpose flour

⅓ to ½ cup dry sherry

½ cup frozen peas, defrosted

1 small box of biscuit mix, such as Jiffy, or measured mix for 8 drop biscuits (make to package directions)

¼ cup finely chopped fresh flat-leaf parsley leaves

1 teaspoon paprika

meat-free blt spaghetti with butter lettuce, leek & tomato

Bring a large pot of water to a boil, salt the water, and cook the spaghetti to 1 minute shy of al dente. ■ Meanwhile, chop and reserve 1 head of lettuce, then chop the second head and add to a food processor with the parsley, basil or tarragon, mint, nuts, cheese, salt and pepper to taste, and the lemon zest. Pulse-chop the greens, then turn on the processor and stream in ¼ cup of the EVOO to form a pesto. Add an extra tablespoon or two if necessary to reach the desired consistency. Transfer to a large pasta serving bowl and reserve. ■ Heat the 2 tablespoons of EVOO in a skillet over medium heat, then add the leeks and garlic. Sauté for 3 minutes, or until the leeks are wilted. Add the grape tomatoes, stir, raise the heat a bit, and place the lid on the pan. Cook for 8 to 10 minutes to burst the tomatoes; force the last few along with a potato masher or wooden spoon if you get impatient. Season with salt and pepper, stir in the wine, and cook off for 1 minute. ■ When the pasta is almost al dente, add a ladle of starchy pasta water to the pesto, then drain the pasta. Add the pasta to the pesto in the bowl along with the tomatoes and leeks, toss for 1 minute, then adjust the salt and pepper to taste. Douse the pasta with the juice of the lemon half and garnish with the reserved chopped lettuce. Serve with extra cheese for topping.

SERVES 4 TO 6

Salt

1 pound spaghetti

2 heads of butter lettuce

½ cup fresh flat-leaf parsley leaves

½ cup fresh basil tops or ¼ cup tarragon leaves

¼ cup fresh mint leaves

¼ cup lightly toasted pine nuts or slivered almonds

A generous handful of grated Parmigiano-Reggiano cheese, plus more for garnish

Black pepper

2 teaspoons grated lemon zest

¼ to ⅓ cup EVOO (extra-virgin olive oil), plus 2 tablespoons

3 to 4 leeks, halved lengthwise, thinly sliced into half-moons on an angle, cleaned, and dried

3 to 4 garlic cloves, grated or chopped

1 pint grape tomatoes

½ cup dry white wine

Juice of ½ lemon

autumn harvest chili

SERVES 4

2 cups vegetable stock

1 large or 2 small dried ancho chile peppers, **stems and seeds removed**

2 small butternut squash, **halved lengthwise, seeded**

5 tablespoons EVOO (extra-virgin olive oil), **divided**

Salt **and** pepper

½ pound cremini mushrooms, **quartered**

1 medium onion, **chopped**

2 garlic cloves, **finely chopped or grated**

1 medium red bell pepper, **seeded and chopped**

2 small zucchini, **cut into ½-inch dice**

1 teaspoon dried marjoram **or oregano, ⅓ palmful**

1 scant tablespoon sweet smoked paprika, **a light palmful**

2½ to 3 tablespoons chili powder, **a couple of rounded palmfuls**

1 (10-ounce) box frozen corn **or 3 ears of corn on the cob, shucked, kernels scraped**

1 (14-ounce) can black beans, **drained**

3 tablespoons tomato paste

1 cup Negra Modelo or other **beer of choice**

1 healthy tablespoon honey

2 cups shredded yellow cheddar cheese

Preheat the oven to 425°F. ■ Place the stock and the ancho in a small pot over low heat. Steep to soften the chile. ■ Place the butternut squash on a baking sheet, drizzle with about 2 tablespoons of the EVOO, and season with salt and pepper. Turn the cut side down and roast the squash in the oven until tender, about 45 minutes. Turn upright for the last 15 minutes to brown at the edges. Once the squash is roasted, remove it from the oven, then turn on the broiler. ■ While the squash is in the oven, place a Dutch oven or large high-sided skillet over medium-high heat with the remaining 3 tablespoons of EVOO. Add the mushrooms and brown for 5 minutes, then add the onions, garlic, bell pepper, and zucchini, season with salt and pepper, and cook until the veggies are tender, 8 to 10 minutes. ■ Puree the softened ancho chile pepper in a food processor or blender with the stock. ■ Add the spices, corn, black beans, and tomato paste to the vegetables in the Dutch oven and cook until heated through, 1 to 2 minutes. Add the beer, stir, add the ancho mixture and the honey, then simmer over low heat until ready to serve. ■ Scoop the finished chili into and over the butternut squash halves—the squash halves serving as bowls—and cover the mounded chili with cheese. Place the chili-filled squash under the broiler to melt the cheese, 2 to 3 minutes, then serve.

I often get requests for more **vegetarian recipes** that are hearty enough to please meat eaters as well. Whether you're a meat eater or not, here's a crowd-pleaser either way.

carbonara with saffron

Bring a large pot of water to a boil, salt the water, and cook the pasta to al dente. Heads up: Just before draining, reserve a ladle of starchy cooking water. ■ While the pasta water comes to a boil, place the saffron in a small pot with the chicken stock. Bring the stock to a gentle boil over medium-high heat, then reduce the heat to a simmer and allow the saffron to steep in the stock as it reduces. ■ Meanwhile, heat the EVOO in a large skillet over medium heat. Add the pancetta and cook until just about crisp, 4 to 5 minutes. Add the garlic, stir for a minute or two more, then stir in the wine and turmeric. ■ Beat the egg yolks with a ladle of starchy cooking water. Drain the pasta and add to the skillet with the pancetta and garlic. Pour the saffron stock over the pasta, toss to combine, and season with pepper. Turn off the heat, then add the tempered eggs, a couple handfuls of cheese, and the parsley. Toss for 2 minutes to form a thick, golden sauce. Toss the spaghetti to coat evenly. Pass extra cheese at the table.

SERVES 4

Salt

1 pound linguine, tagliatelle, or egg tagliatelle

¼ teaspoon saffron, about 2 pinches

1½ cups chicken stock

3 tablespoons EVOO (extra-virgin olive oil)

⅓ pound pancetta, cut as thick as bacon from the deli counter, chopped into ¼-inch dice

4 garlic cloves, grated or finely chopped

½ cup dry white wine

2 teaspoons ground turmeric

3 egg yolks

Black pepper

½ to ⅔ cup grated Pecorino Romano cheese, plus some to pass at the table

A generous handful of finely chopped fresh flat-leaf parsley

pesto-presto chicken

3 tablespoons pine nuts

8 to 10 fresh basil leaves, about ½ cup

¼ cup fresh flat-leaf parsley leaves, a handful

1 (5.4-ounce) round of Boursin garlic and herb soft cheese

½ cup grated Parmigiano-Reggiano cheese, a couple of handfuls

Salt and pepper

4 pieces of boneless skinless chicken breast (6 ounces each)

12 (½-inch-thick) slices of vine-ripened tomato, from about 3 medium tomatoes

2 tablespoons EVOO (extra-virgin olive oil)

Preheat the oven to 450°F. ■ In a small pan over medium heat, lightly toast the pine nuts, then set aside to cool. In the bowl of a food processor, combine the basil, parsley, pine nuts, Boursin cheese, and ¼ cup of the Parmigiano. Season with a little salt and pepper and process into a smooth mixture. ■ Butterfly each piece of chicken breast by slicing into but not all the way through the breast at the equator. Open the two halves as if you were opening a book. Pound the split breasts with a meat mallet to about ¼-inch thickness. Season both sides of the chicken with salt and pepper, then divide the herb-cheese mixture among the four pieces of chicken using a couple of small spoons. Fold the chicken in half (like closing a book) to enclose the cheese mixture. ■ Transfer the chicken to a nonstick rimmed baking sheet and shingle 3 slices of tomato over each breast. Drizzle the stuffed breasts with about 2 tablespoons of EVOO and sprinkle with the remaining Parmigiano. ■ Bake the chicken until it's cooked through and light golden brown, about 20 minutes.

parmigiano-reggiano-crusted
chicken piccata

SERVES 4

4 pieces of boneless skinless chicken breast (6 ounces each)

¼ cup all-purpose flour, for dredging

1 egg, beaten

1 cup shredded Parmigiano-Reggiano cheese, plus a handful or two to toss with the pasta

3 tablespoons EVOO (extra-virgin olive oil)

4 large peeled garlic cloves, grated or mashed to a paste

12 caperberries, thinly sliced, or 3 tablespoons capers in brine, drained and patted dry

2 lemons, 1 very thinly sliced, 1 halved

½ cup dry white wine (eyeball it)

¼ cup chopped fresh flat-leaf parsley

Salt

½ pound angel hair pasta

½ cup chicken stock

2 tablespoons cold butter, cut into small pieces

¼ pound baby spinach leaves, 3 to 4 handfuls

Black pepper

Bring a large pot of water to a boil for the pasta. While the water is heating, pound the chicken with a mallet or a small skillet between sheets of wax paper or plastic wrap to ¼ inch thick. Dredge the chicken in the flour, coat in the egg, then press and coat with the cup of cheese. ■ Heat 2 tablespoons of the EVOO in a large nonstick skillet over medium to medium-high heat. Cook the chicken for 4 to 5 minutes on each side until deeply golden in color. Transfer the chicken to a rack on a baking sheet. Add 1 more tablespoon of EVOO, then the garlic, sliced caperberries or capers, and thinly sliced lemon. Sauté for 2 minutes, then stir in the wine, reduce for a minute, then lower the heat to simmer/low. Add the parsley. ■ When the pasta water comes to a boil, add salt and cook the pasta to al dente, about 3 minutes. Heads up: You will need to reserve a ladle of cooking water before draining. ■ Add the chicken stock to the lemon-caper sauce and stir for 1 minute, then add the cold butter and melt it into the sauce. Add the juice of 1 lemon to the pan. Place the chicken on a platter and spoon a little sauce over it. To the remaining sauce, add the spinach and wilt it in. Add the reserved ladle of starchy cooking water to the sauce, drain the pasta, and toss with the sauce and spinach for 1 minute. Season the pasta with salt and pepper and a little cheese, and serve alongside the chicken.

pork &
black-eyed-pea chili

In a large heavy pot, heat the oil over medium-high heat. Add the sausage and brown for a couple minutes, then add the pork and brown and crumble it for another couple minutes. Add the onions, celery, bell pepper, garlic, bay leaf, and salt and pepper to taste. Cook to soften the vegetables, 5 to 6 minutes. Add the thyme, spices, stock, tomatoes, black-eyed peas, and hot sauce. Stir, bring to a bubble, then reduce the heat and cook for 10 to 12 minutes more. Discard the bay leaf. Serve in shallow bowls. Top the bowls of chili with the scallions and toaster corn muffins or crumbled toasted split muffins.

SERVES 4

1 tablespoon vegetable oil

½ pound andouille sausage, chopped or crumbled

1 pound ground pork

1 onion, chopped

2 to 3 celery stalks from the heart with leafy tops, chopped

1 green bell pepper, seeded and chopped

2 to 3 garlic cloves, chopped

1 bay leaf, fresh or dried

Salt and pepper

A few sprigs of fresh thyme, leaves removed and chopped

1 tablespoon sweet smoked paprika, a palmful

2 tablespoons chili powder

2 teaspoons ground coriander, ⅔ palmful

2 cups chicken stock

1 (14-ounce can) petite diced tomatoes or diced tomatoes with mild chiles

1 (14-ounce) can black-eyed peas, drained

2 tablespoons hot sauce

2 scallions, chopped

4 toaster corn muffins or 2 corn muffins, split and toasted, buttered

whole-wheat penne pasta
& cauliflower

Heat a large pot of water to a boil for the pasta, salt the water, and cook the pasta to al dente. ■ Trim the cauliflower and chop it into small florets. Heat the EVOO in a large skillet with a lid or in a Dutch oven over medium to medium-high heat. ■ If using pancetta, cook it for a couple of minutes to crisp the pancetta and render its fat. ■ Add the onions, rosemary, and garlic, then stir and add the florets. Season with salt, pepper, and a little nutmeg. Cover the pan and cook for 7 to 8 minutes, stirring occasionally. ■ When the cauliflower is just about tender, remove the lid, add the wine, and cook down for a minute or so. Add the stock, reduce the heat, and cover until the pasta is ready. ■ Drain the pasta, toss with the cauliflower mixture and cheese, and adjust the seasonings to taste. ■ Garnish shallow bowls of pasta and cauliflower with a sprig of rosemary.

SERVES 4

Salt

1 pound whole-wheat penne

1 head of cauliflower

2 tablespoons EVOO **(extra-virgin olive oil)**

¼ pound pancetta, **cut into fine dice (optional)**

1 onion, **finely chopped**

2 to 3 sprigs of fresh rosemary, **leaves removed and finely chopped (about 2 tablespoons)**

3 large garlic cloves, **chopped**

Black pepper

Freshly grated nutmeg

½ cup dry white wine

1 cup chicken stock

1 cup grated Pecorino Romano **cheese or super-sharp white cheddar cheese**

steakhouse chili pot

1 tablespoon EVOO (extra-virgin olive oil)

4 slices lean, smoky bacon, finely chopped

2 pounds coarse-ground sirloin

1 large onion, finely chopped

3 to 4 garlic cloves, finely chopped

4 tablespoons chili powder, preferably Gerhardt's brand

Salt and pepper

1 (14-ounce) can tomato sauce

⅓ cup Worcestershire sauce

¼ cup dark brown sugar

2 tablespoons hot sauce

2 cups beef stock

Sour cream, for topping

½ cup finely chopped fresh flat-leaf parsley leaves

Heat the EVOO in a chili pot over medium-high to high heat. Add the bacon and cook it for a couple minutes to render its fat. Add the beef and cook until brown, 5 to 6 minutes, stirring occasionally to break up the lumps. Add the onions, garlic, chili powder, a little salt, and lots of black pepper, and cook to soften for 5 minutes. In a bowl, stir together the tomato sauce, Worcestershire sauce, brown sugar, and hot sauce. Add the sauce to the chili pot to combine, then add the stock, bring to a boil, reduce the heat, and cook to thicken for 6 to 7 minutes.
■ Serve shallow bowls of chili with sour cream and lots of parsley on top.

This chili tastes like **a steakhouse meal in a bowl**: bacon, beef, steak sauce, and sour cream. Loosen your belts. **Serve with a spinach salad.**

cherry tomato & ravioli soup

In a large, deep skillet with a tight-fitting lid or a Dutch oven, heat the EVOO over medium-high heat. Add the cherry tomatoes and stir, then add the garlic and salt and pepper to taste, cover the pan, and cook for 7 to 8 minutes, shaking occasionally until the tomatoes burst and a thick sauce forms. Add the stock and 2 cups water and bring to a boil for a couple of minutes. Add the ravioli and cook for 3 to 4 minutes or until the ravioli are tender. Turn off the heat, wilt in the basil leaves, and stir in the scallions. Serve in shallow bowls and garnish with large shavings of cheese made with a vegetable peeler or hand grater. Serve with crusty bread for dunking.

SERVES 4

2 tablespoons EVOO (extra-virgin olive oil)

2 pints cherry tomatoes

2 garlic cloves, **crushed or chopped**

Salt and pepper

1 quart chicken stock

1 pound fresh cheese ravioli

1 cup fresh basil leaves

2 scallions, **white and green parts, chopped** (reserve some for garnish)

A chunk of Parmigiano-Reggiano cheese

Crusty bread, **for dunking**

pimiento mac 'n' cheese

SERVES 6

Salt

1 pound cavatappi pasta **(hollow, fat corkscrew-shaped pasta) or pasta elbows**

1 tablespoon EVOO **(extra-virgin olive oil)**

3 tablespoons butter

1 medium onion**, finely chopped**

3 garlic cloves**, finely chopped**

Black pepper

3 tablespoons all-purpose flour

2 tablespoons sweet paprika**, plus additional for garnish**

2 cups whole milk

2 teaspoons hot sauce

3 cups grated sharp yellow cheddar cheese

2 (4-ounce) jars pimientos**, drained**

¼ cup finely chopped fresh flat-leaf or curly parsley

Bring a large pot of water to a boil for the pasta. Salt the water and cook the pasta to just shy of al dente. ■ Heat a large pot over medium heat with the EVOO and butter. When the butter melts, add the onions, garlic, and salt and pepper and cook until the onions are softened, about 5 minutes. Add the flour and cook for another minute. Stir in the paprika. Whisk in the milk and hot sauce and bring up to a bubble, then cook to thicken for a minute or two. Turn off the heat and stir in half of the cheese in a figure-eight motion until melted. Add the pimentos. ■ Preheat the broiler. ■ When the pasta is nearly al dente, drain it well and add it to the pot with the cheese sauce. Toss to combine. Then pour the pasta into a baking dish, top with the remaining cheese, and brown it under the broiler, 2 to 3 minutes. Garnish with the chopped parsley and a generous sprinkle of sweet paprika.

Serve with a mixed green salad dressed with oil and vinegar.

cobb pasta toss

Preheat the oven to 400°F. Place a large pot of water over high heat to boil. ■ Scatter the tomatoes onto a rimmed baking sheet and drizzle with about 2 tablespoons of EVOO and some salt and pepper. Toss lightly to coat and roast them in the hot oven until they burst open and are tender, 12 to 15 minutes. Place the bacon on a broiler pan and transfer to the oven as well. Cook until crispy, about 15 minutes. ■ While the tomatoes and bacon are in the oven, salt the boiling water, drop in the pasta, and cook to al dente according to the package directions. When the pasta is ready, reserve a large mug of the starchy cooking water, then drain the pasta and return it to the pot it was cooked in. ■ While the pasta is cooking, season the chicken pieces with salt and pepper. Heat a large skillet with 1 tablespoon of the EVOO, add the chicken, and sauté until golden brown and cooked through, about 6 minutes. ■ While the chicken is cooking, place the diced avocado into a small bowl and squeeze the juice of the lemon over it, tossing to coat. ■ When the chicken is finished cooking, add the garlic to the pan, cook for 1 minute, then sprinkle in a few dashes of hot sauce and toss to coat. ■ In a large serving bowl, add the cooked tomatoes and the scallions, then add the reserved pasta water and pasta. Mash the tomatoes. Top with the chicken, crumble the cooked bacon over the top, and toss with the avocado, blue cheese, basil, and parsley.

SERVES 4

- 3 pints grape or cherry tomatoes
- 3 tablespoons EVOO (extra-virgin olive oil), divided
- Salt and pepper
- 6 slices bacon
- 1 pound penne or whole-wheat penne pasta
- 1 pound boneless skinless chicken breasts, cut into bite-size pieces
- 2 avocados, pitted and diced
- 1 lemon
- 2 garlic cloves, grated or finely chopped
- A few dashes of hot sauce
- 4 to 5 scallions, thinly sliced on the bias
- 1 cup blue cheese crumbles
- ¼ cup fresh basil, a handful, chopped
- ¼ cup fresh flat-leaf parsley, a handful, chopped

Pizzoccheri is a classic combo that is a **hearty fall fave** of mine: buckwheat pasta, potatoes, cabbage, butter, and sage. Here's a quick, easy spin on it.

cabbage & hay pasta

Bring a large pot of water to a boil, salt it, and add the spaghetti and the potatoes. Cook until the spaghetti is al dente and the potatoes are just tender, about 10 minutes. Drain. (Alternatively, if using fresh buckwheat pasta, start the potatoes first, cook for 8 minutes, then add the pasta and cook for 2 to 3 minutes more.) ■ Cut the cabbage into 2 pieces. Cut away the core and shred the cabbage carefully with a sharp knife. ■ While the pasta is cooking, in a large skillet, heat the EVOO over medium heat. Add the cabbage, onions, and garlic, then season with salt and pepper. Cook until tender, about 10 minutes. Stir in the chicken stock and simmer for 5 minutes. ■ In a small skillet, melt the butter over medium-low heat. Add the sage leaves and cook until crisp, 3 to 4 minutes. ■ Toss the pasta and potatoes with the cabbage mixture. Add the sage leaves and butter and the cheese, and toss well.

SERVES 4 TO 6

Salt

1 pound whole-wheat spaghetti **or fresh** buckwheat pasta

2 starchy potatoes, **peeled and cut into small cubes**

½ head of green cabbage

2 tablespoons EVOO **(extra-virgin olive oil)**

1 large onion, **thinly sliced**

3 garlic cloves, **grated or chopped**

Black pepper

1 cup chicken or vegetable stock

4 tablespoons (½ stick) butter, **cut into pieces**

12 large fresh sage leaves

½ cup grated Parmigiano-Reggiano cheese, **a couple generous handfuls**

french onion & wild mushroom soup

SERVES 4

4 tablespoons (½ stick) butter

2 tablespoons EVOO (extra-virgin olive oil)

3 large onions, thinly sliced

1 bay leaf, fresh or dried

1½ teaspoons dried thyme, ½ palmful

Salt and pepper

1 quart beef or chicken stock

1 ounce mixed dried wild mushrooms or porcini mushrooms

⅓ to ½ cup dry sherry or dry white wine (eyeball it)

4 thick slices crusty bread

1 large garlic clove

½ pound Gruyère cheese, shredded

In a heavy soup pot, melt the butter in the EVOO over medium-high heat. Add the onions, bay leaf, and thyme, then season with salt and pepper. Cook for 25 minutes, or until the onions are softened and browned. ■ Meanwhile, in a large saucepan, bring the stock, dried mushrooms, and 2 cups water to a boil. Lower the heat and simmer for 15 minutes. Using a slotted spoon, transfer the mushrooms to a work surface, then chop. ■ Preheat the broiler. Pour the sherry into the onion mixture and cook over medium heat, scraping up any browned bits. Stir in the mushrooms and the hot stock. ■ Toast the bread under the broiler, rub with the garlic, and cover with the cheese. Broil until the cheese is melted and browned, 2 to 3 minutes. ■ Discard the bay leaf. Ladle the soup into bowls and top with the toasts.

salad-a-ghetti

Place a large pot of water over high heat to boil for the pasta. When the water reaches a bubble, salt it and drop in the pasta. Cook to al dente according to the package directions and drain. (Heads up: Save a large mug of starchy cooking water to use when cooking the filling.) Reserve. ■ While the pasta is cooking, place a large skillet over low heat with the EVOO. Add the garlic and thyme to the pan and cook until the garlic is tender and very aromatic, 5 to 6 minutes. Increase the heat to medium-high and add the reserved starchy cooking water and the cooked pasta. Add the frisée, arugula, radicchio, lemon juice, Parmigiano, and a good sprinkle of salt and pepper to the pan and cook, tossing frequently, until the veggies have wilted and the pasta has absorbed the water, 2 to 3 minutes. Sprinkle with the parsley and serve.

SERVES 4

Salt

1 pound spaghetti

4 tablespoons EVOO (extra-virgin olive oil)

5 to 6 garlic cloves, **finely chopped or grated**

2 teaspoons fresh thyme leaves

1 small head of frisée lettuce, **stemmed and cleaned (about 2 cups)**

2 cups baby arugula

½ small head of radicchio, **shredded (about 1 cup)**

Juice of 1 lemon

¼ cup grated Parmigiano-Reggiano cheese, a handful

Black pepper

3 tablespoons chopped fresh flat-leaf parsley **leaves**

cure-a-cold
spring chicken soup

SERVES 4

2 pieces boneless skinless chicken breast **(6 ounces each)**

2 onions, **1 halved and 1 chopped**

2 garlic cloves, **crushed**

1 bay leaf, **fresh or dried**

2 tablespoons EVOO **(extra-virgin olive oil)**

3 small to medium carrots, **peeled and chopped or thinly sliced**

4 small celery stalks, **finely chopped**

Salt **and** black pepper

1 quart chicken stock

⅓ pound wide egg noodles

4 scallions, thinly sliced on an angle

¼ cup finely chopped fresh flat-leaf parsley

¼ cup chopped fresh dill

Zest and juice of 1 lemon

In a sauce pot, combine the chicken, halved onion, garlic, bay leaf, and enough water to cover. Bring to a boil, then lower the heat and simmer gently until the chicken is cooked through, 15 to 20 minutes. ■ Meanwhile, in a soup pot or Dutch oven, heat the EVOO over medium heat. Add the chopped onion, carrots, and celery; season with salt and pepper. Cover the pot and cook until the vegetables are softened, about 8 minutes. Add the chicken stock and bring to a boil. ■ Remove the poached chicken from the liquid and add about 2 cups of liquids, poured through a strainer, to the soup pot. Dice the poached chicken, then stir in the egg noodles, add the chicken, and simmer for 5 minutes. Turn off the heat and stir in the scallions, parsley, dill, and lemon zest and juice. Season the soup with salt and pepper to taste.

If you feel a cold coming on, take your vitamins, drink lots of fluids, and make a pot of this.

1 cozy food

2 make your own takeout

Quicker than you can call, wait for, and serve up take-out food, you can make it instead. When you make your own takeout-style foods, you control the salt, the fat, and the quality of the ingredients. You can feel better about eating foods that you might otherwise feel guilty about eating too often or too much of. This style of recipe—Thai It You'll Like It Hot Curry Beef Noodle Bowls on page 94 and Chinese Orange-Barbecue Cashew Chicken on page 102—can make for fun and affordable menu choices for casual entertaining as well. Whether you're excited to watch one of your favorite movies tonight or a couple of buddies are coming by, try making *your* own takeout and save on the tip!

3 fancy fake-outs

thai it you'll like it hot curry
beef noodle bowls

SERVES 4

1¼ to 1½ pounds flank steak

Salt

1 pound whole-grain or whole-wheat spaghetti

5 to 6 ounces shiitake mushrooms

1 red bell pepper

1 hot red chile pepper

2 tablespoons high-temp oil such as peanut, canola, or safflower

3 tablespoons curry paste, such as Patak's, mild to medium heat

3 to 4 garlic cloves, grated or chopped

4 to 5 scallions, cut into 1-inch-long pieces

3 tablespoons fish sauce

2 cups chicken stock

1 cup frozen shelled edamame

1 loosely packed cup fresh basil leaves, thinly sliced or torn

Zest and juice of 1 lime

Black pepper

Place the flank steak in the freezer for a few minutes to aid in thinly slicing it safely. ■ Bring a large pot of water to a boil, salt the water, and cook the pasta to al dente. ■ While the pasta water comes to a boil, stem and thinly slice the mushrooms, seed and thinly slice the bell and hot peppers. ■ Remove the meat from the freezer and thinly slice into ¼-inch-wide, 2-inch-long pieces. ■ In a large skillet or wok, heat the oil over medium heat with the curry paste for 1 to 2 minutes. Raise the heat to medium high. Add the beef and cook in a single layer for 2 to 3 minutes, then flip the meat and add the shiitakes, garlic, bell and hot peppers, and scallions. Stir-fry for 2 to 3 minutes more, then add the fish sauce and stock and bring to a boil. Add the edamame, heat through for a minute, then add the basil. ■ Drain the pasta. Place in individual bowls, then add the steak, vegetables, and broth. Sprinkle the lime zest and juice over the mixture, toss vigorously, and season with black pepper to taste.

For a refreshing, **nothing-to-it dessert**, pair this menu with **Green Melon with Lime and Lemon Sorbet** (page 302).

sirloin burgers with garlic–black pepper–parmesan sauce & roasted tomatoes with basil & balsamic drizzle

Preheat the oven to 325°F. ■ Place a cooling rack over a rimmed baking sheet. Arrange the tomatoes on the rack, then drizzle with a touch of EVOO and season the tomato slices with salt and pepper. Roast the tomatoes for 45 minutes, or until tender and caramelized. Set aside. ■ When the tomatoes are about ready, place a large skillet over medium-high heat with the 2 tablespoons of EVOO. While the pan is heating up, combine the sirloin with some salt and pepper. Form the mixture into 4 patties thicker at the edges and thinner in the center for even cooking and to ensure you end up with a flat burger (the burgers will bulge up during cooking). Cook the patties for 10 minutes for medium-rare, turning once. Cook for 12 minutes for pink centers and 14 minutes for well-done. ■ While the patties are cooking, place a small pot over medium heat with the butter. Add the garlic to the melted butter and cook for about 1 minute. Add the flour to the pan and cook for 1 minute more. Season with salt and the coarse black pepper. Whisk the milk into the butter-flour mixture and bring up to a bubble. Simmer until the sauce has thickened, about 2 minutes. Stir in the grated cheese. Prepare a balsamic drizzle in a small pot if not using store-bought. ■ To assemble, place some lettuce on each bun bottom and top it with a burger patty. Pour garlic–black pepper–Parmesan sauce over the top, set the roasted tomatoes in the sauce, scatter basil over the tomatoes, and garnish with balsamic drizzle. Set the bun tops in place and serve.

SERVES 4

3 vine-ripened tomatoes, **sliced about ¼ inch thick**

2 tablespoons EVOO (extra-virgin olive oil), **plus more for drizzling**

Salt and pepper, **plus 1 teaspoon coarse black pepper**

2 pounds coarse-ground sirloin

3 tablespoons butter

2 garlic cloves, **finely chopped or grated**

2 tablespoons all-purpose flour

1 cup whole milk

½ cup grated Parmigiano-Reggiano cheese

Balsamic drizzle, **store-bought, or reduce ½ cup balsamic vinegar with 3 tablespoons brown sugar over medium heat until thick and syrupy, a couple minutes**

7 to 8 red leaf or red romaine lettuce **leaves, shredded**

4 kaiser rolls, **toasted**

½ cup fresh basil leaves, **8 to 10 leaves, thinly sliced**

EQUIPMENT NOTE You'll need a cooling rack to roast your tomatoes. Ask your butcher to freshly grind the sirloin on the coarse setting. If a butcher is not available, buy one pound each of ground chuck and ground sirloin and combine them.

cherry tomato red clam sauce
with linguine

SERVES 6

Salt

1 pound linguine

3 tablespoons EVOO (extra-virgin olive oil)

5 to 6 anchovies

1 red onion, **finely chopped**

4 garlic cloves, **chopped**

1 pint small cherry tomatoes

½ teaspoon crushed red pepper flakes

2 sprigs of oregano, **leaves stripped and finely chopped**

A handful of fresh flat-leaf parsley leaves, **finely chopped**

Black pepper

1 cup dry white wine

3 tablespoons butter, **cut into small pieces**

3 pounds Manila clams, **scrubbed**

½ cup fresh basil leaves, **torn**

Bring a large pot of water to a boil, salt the water, and cook the pasta to just shy of al dente. ■ While the water comes to a boil, heat the EVOO in a large pot over medium to medium-high heat. Add the anchovies and melt them into the oil. Add the onions, garlic, and tomatoes to the pot and season with the red pepper flakes, oregano, parsley, and black pepper to taste. Sauté until the tomatoes burst and the onions are soft, 8 to 10 minutes. Add the wine and reduce for 1 to 2 minutes, then melt the butter into the sauce and add the clams. Cover the pot and cook the clams until they open, 6 to 7 minutes. Discard any unopened clams and add the pasta to the pot. Toss the linguine with the sauce for 2 to 3 minutes so the pasta absorbs the flavors. Add the basil, taste to adjust the seasonings, and serve.

fennel-pepper spaghetti

Bring a large pot of water to a boil over high heat. Salt the water and cook the pasta to al dente. ■ While the pasta is cooking, place a large skillet over medium-high heat with the EVOO. Add the fennel seed, toast for a minute, then add the onions and peppers and cook for 5 minutes. Stir in the garlic and red pepper flakes, season with salt and black pepper, and cook for 3 more minutes, then stir in the tomatoes, breaking them up with a wooden spoon or potato masher. Stir in the stock and simmer the sauce to thicken while the pasta cooks. When the pasta is almost done, stir most of the basil and parsley into the sauce, saving a little for garnish. ■ Drain the pasta and return it to the hot pot with the butter and cheese and the sauce, then toss to combine. Serve the pasta in shallow bowls and sprinkle with the remaining herbs.

SERVES 4

Salt

1 pound spaghetti

¼ cup EVOO (extra-virgin olive oil)

2 teaspoons fennel seed

1 red onion, **quartered, then thinly sliced**

1 red bell pepper, **quartered lengthwise, seeded, and thinly sliced**

2 cubanelle peppers (Italian frying peppers), **quartered lengthwise, seeded, and thinly sliced**

3 garlic cloves, **finely chopped or grated**

½ teaspoon crushed red pepper flakes

Black pepper

1 (28-ounce) can San Marzano tomatoes

1 cup chicken or vegetable stock

½ cup fresh basil leaves, **torn or thinly sliced**

¼ cup chopped fresh flat-leaf parsley leaves

2 tablespoons butter, **cut into small pieces**

½ cup grated Parmigiano-Reggiano cheese

chinese orange-barbecue
cashew chicken

SERVES 4

3 tablespoons canola or vegetable oil

1½ pounds boneless skinless chicken breasts or thighs, chopped into bite-size pieces

Salt and pepper

1 red bell pepper, chopped into ½-inch dice

1 onion, chopped into ½-inch dice

2 to 3 garlic cloves, finely chopped or grated

1 inch of fresh gingerroot, peeled and grated or finely chopped

¼ cup hoisin sauce

¼ cup orange marmalade

1 tablespoon hot sauce

2 tablespoons tamari (aged soy sauce)

½ cup chicken stock

½ cup honey-roasted cashews

4 scallions, thinly sliced on the bias

Place a large skillet over high heat with about 2 tablespoons of the oil. When the pan is very hot, add the meat, season with salt and pepper, and stir-fry until golden brown, 4 to 5 minutes. Remove the meat from the pan and reserve on a plate. ■ Add the remaining tablespoon of oil, then add the bell pepper, onion, garlic, and ginger to the skillet and stir-fry for 3 minutes, or until crisp-tender. ■ In a small bowl, stir together the hoisin sauce, orange marmalade, hot sauce, tamari, and stock. ■ Return the chicken to the skillet and pour in the sauce. Add the cashews, toss to coat, and continue cooking until the sauce thickens up, about 1 minute more. ■ Serve the stir-fry with brown rice and garnish with the scallions.

Serve with **brown or light brown rice** cooked to the package directions for four servings.

real-deal rellenos

SERVES 4

8 poblano peppers

½ cup walnuts

2 cups heavy cream

2 teaspoons grated orange zest

Salt and pepper

2 tablespoons EVOO (extra-virgin olive oil)

2 pounds ground pork **or beef**

1 onion, **chopped**

4 garlic cloves, **finely chopped or grated**

2 teaspoons ground cumin

2 teaspoons smoked paprika

½ teaspoon ground cinnamon

2 tablespoons tomato paste

¼ cup raisins, **a handful**

1 cup beef stock

FESTIVE NOTE Garnish with pomegranate seeds after you take the rellenos out of the oven and just before serving. This is a traditional garnish for this type of relleno.

Preheat the broiler. ■ Place the poblanos on a rimmed baking sheet and char under the broiler, flipping as each side blackens, until the entire pepper is blackened, about 3 minutes on each side. Heads up: Leave the oven door open a crack to allow steam to escape as the peppers cook. The peppers may also be charred over an open flame on a gas stovetop. While the charred peppers are still hot, transfer them to a large bowl and cover with plastic wrap. Let the peppers steam until the skin is loose and the peppers can be handled, about 5 minutes. Peel the skin from the peppers and cut each one open with a single slice from the stem to the base. Carefully scoop out the seeds of the pepper, maintaining the pepper's entire shape. Reserve the peppers. ■ When the peppers are removed from the broiler, turn the oven to 400°F. In a skillet over medium heat, toast the walnuts until they're aromatic and golden brown, about 5 minutes. When they are toasted, put them in a food processor and pulse until they're ground. ■ In a small pot over medium heat, combine the cream, ground toasted walnuts, orange zest, and salt and pepper. Bring the liquid up to a bubble and then reduce the heat to medium and simmer until the cream has thickened, about 5 minutes. ■ While the cream is working, place a large skillet over medium-high heat with the EVOO, add the meat, and cook the meat for 5 minutes, stirring occasionally to break up the lumps. Add the onions and garlic to the pan and cook until the onions are tender, 4 to 5 minutes more. Stir in the cumin, smoked paprika, cinnamon, tomato paste, raisins, beef stock, and salt and pepper. Cook the mixture until the liquid has reduced and has thickened, about 1 minute. ■ Fill the poblanos with the meat filling and arrange them in a serving dish or in individual shallow bowls. Top with thickened cream sauce and serve with rice.

Serve with **white rice** or with **Brown Rice with Orange** (page 272).

chicken parm pasta toss

Bring a large pot of water to a boil for the pasta. Salt the water and cook the pasta to al dente. Heads up: Before draining, reserve a cup of the starchy cooking liquid. ■ While the water is coming up to a boil, place a large skillet over medium-high heat with the EVOO. Season the chicken pieces with the poultry seasoning, salt, and pepper, then add to the hot skillet. Cook the chicken until it's golden brown and cooked through, 4 minutes per side. ■ Once the chicken is brown, add the onions to the pan, and cook until softened, about 5 minutes. Add the garlic, then cook for a couple minutes more. Add the tomatoes and cover the pan with a lid. Cook, stirring occasionally, until the tomatoes burst open and begin to release their juices, about 6 or 7 minutes. Use a wooden spoon to mash or crush any tomatoes that do not burst on their own. Season the sauce with salt and pepper. ■ Add the drained pasta and reserved starchy cooking water to the skillet, toss for 1 minute, and turn off the heat. Add the basil, arugula, and cheese and toss for a minute more, then serve in shallow bowls.

SERVES 4

Salt

1 pound whole-wheat penne pasta

3 tablespoons EVOO **(extra-virgin olive oil)**

1 pound boneless skinless chicken breasts **or thighs, chopped into bite-size pieces**

2 teaspoons poultry seasoning

Black pepper

1 medium red onion, **chopped**

2 to 3 garlic cloves, **finely chopped or grated**

2 pints grape tomatoes

2 cups fresh basil leaves, **chopped**

3 cups arugula **or baby arugula, roughly chopped**

1 cup shredded Parmigiano-Reggiano **cheese**

shish kebabs with spanakopita orzo

Salt

½ **pound** orzo pasta

1 **tablespoon chopped fresh** oregano **or marjoram leaves or 1 teaspoon dried oregano**

5 **tablespoons** EVOO **(extra-virgin olive oil)**

1 **teaspoon** onion powder

1 **teaspoon** garlic powder

Black pepper

2 **pounds** lamb top round **or shoulder steaks, cut into bite-size cubes**

1 **small** onion, **finely chopped**

3 to 4 garlic cloves, **finely chopped or grated**

½ **cup** vegetable stock

3 **cups** spinach, **divided**

1 **cup crumbled** feta cheese

Preheat the broiler or a grill. ■ Bring a large pot of water to a boil over high heat for the pasta. Salt the boiling water and cook the pasta to al dente according to the package directions. Drain the cooked pasta and reserve. ■ While the pasta is cooking, in a large mixing bowl whisk together the oregano, 3 tablespoons of the EVOO, onion powder, garlic powder, and some salt and pepper. Toss the lamb cubes in the mixture to coat. Thread the lamb onto metal skewers (wooden skewers are OK, too, just soak them in water for 20 minutes prior to use). Broil or grill the lamb until seared and cooked to medium, 2 to 3 minutes per side. ■ While the lamb is cooking, prepare the orzo: Place a large skillet over medium-high heat with the remaining 2 tablespoons EVOO. Add the onions and garlic to the pan and sauté until tender, about 5 minutes. ■ While the veggies are cooking, add the vegetable stock and about 2 cups of the spinach to the bowl of a food processor and process until smooth. Add the puree to the onions and garlic to heat through, about 30 seconds. Remove the pan from the heat and stir in the reserved orzo, the remaining whole leaves of spinach, the feta, and some salt and pepper. ■ Serve the shish kebabs over the orzo.

Try with the **Greek Salad with Yogurt Dressing** (page 273) if you need to eat **more vegetables**.

mini crunchy tuna burgers

Place the tuna in a food processor and pulse. Put the ground tuna in a bowl and combine with the garlic, chives, black pepper, and tamari. Place the panko crumbs and sesame seeds in a dish. Form 8 small tuna patties and roll in the bread-crumb mixture. ■ Place a large skillet over medium-high heat with the vegetable oil. Add the burgers to the pan and cook for 2 minutes per side, or until lightly golden brown on the outside and pink in the middle. ■ Place the burgers on the bun bottoms. Top with lettuce, pickled ginger, cucumber, and onion, then slather the bun tops with mustard and set the tops in place. Serve with the fancy root-vegetable chips.

MAKES 8 SLIDER-SIZE BURGERS; SERVES 4

1 pound fresh tuna, **roughly chopped**

3 garlic cloves, **grated or finely chopped**

¼ cup finely chopped fresh chives

Freshly ground black pepper

2 tablespoons tamari **(aged soy sauce)**

1 cup panko **bread crumbs**

2 tablespoons black sesame seeds

¼ cup vegetable, peanut, safflower, or canola oil

8 small dinner rolls **or brioche rolls**

½ head Bibb lettuce, **4 to 5 leaves**

¼ cup pickled ginger

¼ seedless cucumber, **thinly sliced**

1 red onion, **thinly sliced**

½ cup store-bought wasabi mustard **or Asian sweet-hot mustard, or combine in a small bowl**

> **½ cup** yellow mustard

> **2 tablespoons** honey

> **1 teaspoon** wasabi paste

Terra Chips **or other fancy root-vegetable chips**

as you like it
citrus soy stir-fry

Salt

1 pound whole-wheat spaghetti

1 cup orange marmalade

1 inch of fresh gingerroot, **peeled and grated**

1 cup chicken or vegetable stock

½ cup tamari **(aged soy sauce); eyeball it**

1 teaspoon coarse black pepper

1 teaspoon hot sauce

2 tablespoons high-temp oil **such as safflower, peanut, or vegetable**

1 pound thinly sliced chicken **or pork or peeled and deveined shrimp**

1 cup shelled edamame

1 red bell pepper, **seeded and thinly sliced**

¼ pound snow peas, **halved on an angle**

1 small bunch of thin scallions, **thinly sliced on an angle into 2-inch pieces, whites and greens**

Bring a large pot of water to a boil for the pasta. Salt the water and cook the pasta to al dente. ■ Prepare all the ingredients and pile them near the stovetop. ■ Mix together the orange marmalade, ginger, stock, tamari, black pepper, and hot sauce in a bowl. ■ Once the pasta is dropped into the pot, heat the oil in a large nonstick skillet over high heat. When the oil smokes, add the chicken, pork, or shrimp and stir-fry for 1 to 2 minutes, then add the vegetables and stir-fry for 3 minutes more. Stir in the sauce and toss for 1 minute, then drain the pasta and combine. For shrimp, stir-fry it for 1 minute, add the edamame, snow peas, and scallions. Stir-fry for 3 minutes more, then add the sauce and toss with the pasta.

spinach-artichoke
stuffed shells

Preheat the oven to 375°F. ■ Bring a large pot of water to a boil for the pasta. Salt the water and cook the shells to just shy of al dente. ■ While the shells are cooking, in the bottom of a casserole dish mash up the tomatoes, then stir in the basil and melted butter and season with salt and pepper. ■ Place a skillet over medium-high heat with the EVOO. Add the garlic to the pan and stir for 1 minute. Add the spinach and nutmeg to the pan and cook to heat through. Transfer to a large bowl and add the artichokes, egg yolk, ricotta, Parmigiano, lemon zest, thyme, and parsley and season with salt and pepper. Stir and spoon this mixture into the shells and arrange split side up in the sauce. Cover the casserole with foil and transfer to the oven. Bake for 20 minutes, remove the foil, and continue baking until the filling is golden brown, about 15 minutes.

SERVES 4

Salt

20 large pasta shells

1 (28-ounce) can whole San Marzano tomatoes

7 to 8 fresh basil leaves, **torn**

3 tablespoons butter, **melted**

Black pepper

2 tablespoons EVOO (extra-virgin olive oil)

3 garlic cloves, **finely chopped or grated**

1 (10-ounce) box chopped frozen spinach, **defrosted (or ¾ pound fresh young spinach, chopped)**

Freshly grated nutmeg

1 (10-ounce) box frozen baby or regular artichoke hearts, **defrosted and rough chopped**

1 egg yolk

2 cups ricotta cheese

½ cup grated Parmigiano-Reggiano cheese

1 teaspoon grated lemon zest

1 tablespoon fresh thyme leaves, **a few sprigs, chopped**

¼ cup chopped fresh flat-leaf parsley **leaves**

pancetta-wrapped
shrimp all' amatriciana

SERVES 4

Salt

1 pound short cut pasta, **such as penne or farfalle**

24 large shrimp, **peeled and deveined**

Freshly ground black pepper

24 thin slices pancetta

3 tablespoons EVOO **(extra-virgin olive oil)**

1 small sweet onion, **finely chopped**

2 pints cherry tomatoes

¼ cup white wine

5 to 6 fresh basil leaves, **chopped**

½ cup chopped fresh flat-leaf parsley **leaves**

Bring a large pot of water to a boil. Salt the water and cook the pasta to al dente. Drain the water and reserve. ■ While the pasta is cooking, season the shrimp with salt and pepper. Unroll a slice of pancetta into a strip and wrap the strip around a shrimp. Repeat to wrap all of the shrimp. Place a large skillet over medium-high heat with 2 tablespoons of the EVOO. Sear the wrapped shrimp in the pan until they are golden brown and cooked through, 3 to 4 minutes per side. Remove the shrimp from the pan and reserve on a plate. ■ Return the skillet to medium-high heat and add the remaining tablespoon of EVOO. Add the onion to the pan and cook until tender, 2 to 3 minutes. Add the cherry tomatoes and wine to the pan and cover. Continue cooking until the tomatoes begin to burst, about 5 minutes. Help the rest of the tomatoes along by mashing them with a wooden spoon or potato masher. Season the sauce with salt and pepper and stir in the herbs. Toss the cooked pasta with the sauce and divide among 4 plates, topping each with some shrimp.

argentinean surf & turf
skewers with chimichurri

SERVES 4

2-pound marbled beef sirloin about 1½ inches thick, cut into 16 cubes

16 large shrimp, peeled and deveined, tails on

¾ cup EVOO (extra-virgin olive oil)

Salt and pepper

4 teaspoons sweet or sweet smoked paprika

¾ pound Spanish chorizo, casing removed, cut into 16 pieces

1 cup packed fresh flat-leaf parsley leaves

A couple sprigs of rosemary, leaves stripped from stems

½ cup loosely packed fresh sage leaves

2 to 3 sprigs of fresh oregano or marjoram, leaves stripped from stems

1 shallot, chopped

2 large garlic cloves, finely chopped or grated

1 teaspoon crushed red pepper flakes

3 to 4 tablespoons red wine vinegar (eyeball it)

2 lemons, cut into wedges

Preheat a grill or grill pan to medium-high. ■ Place the beef and shrimp into 2 separate bowls and toss each with about 2 tablespoons EVOO, some salt and pepper, and about 2 teaspoons paprika. Thread the beef and chorizo alternately onto metal skewers, placing a chunk of sausage after every 2 cubes of beef. For the shrimp skewers alternate shrimp and chorizo. ■ When the grill is hot, place the beef skewers on first and cook for about 8 minutes for pink meat, turning occasionally. Place the shrimp on the grill a couple minutes later and cook for 5 to 6 minutes, turning occasionally, or until the shrimp are firm. ■ Fill a food processor bowl with the parsley, rosemary, sage, oregano or marjoram, shallots, garlic, red pepper flakes, and red wine vinegar. Pulse the machine to chop up the herbs and then turn it on and stream in about ½ cup EVOO to make a thick herb sauce. Season the condiment with salt and pepper to taste. ■ When the skewers are ready, lay them next to rice and serve with the lemon wedges and the chimichurri.

A **good Argentinean meal** does not go unfinished without **a tasty green chimichurri!** Serve with white or brown rice cooked according to the package directions or try the **Pimiento Rice** on page 275.

stuffed hot sausage
meatball subs

Preheat the oven to 425°F. ■ Arrange a cooling rack on a rimmed baking sheet. Dip your hands in warm water to prevent sticking. Separate the 2 pounds of sausage into 4 equal portions. Each portion should form 3 meatballs. Nest a cube of smoked cheese into the center of each meatball. Coat the meatballs with EVOO and roast on the rack above the baking sheet until firm and cooked through, about 18 minutes. ■ While the meatballs cook, heat the tablespoon of EVOO in a sauce pot over medium heat. Add the onions and garlic and cook until tender, 5 to 6 minutes. Then stir in the olives, sun-dried tomatoes, and tomatoes, season with salt and pepper, and bring to a simmer. ■ Take out the meatballs, turn off the oven, and crisp the rolls for a minute. Split the rolls and fill each with 3 meatballs. Top with some sauce, basil, and cheese and serve.

SERVES 4

2 pounds bulk Italian hot sausage

1 pound smoked mozzarella, **cut into 12 cubes**

EVOO **(extra-virgin olive oil) for drizzling, plus 1 tablespoon**

1 onion, **finely chopped**

2 garlic cloves, **chopped**

¼ cup pitted kalamata black olives, **chopped**

¼ cup softened sun-dried tomatoes, **chopped**

1 (28-ounce) can Italian crushed tomatoes

Salt **and** black pepper

4 crusty sub rolls, ciabatta bread, or individual ciabatta rolls, **7 to 8 inches long per person**

A handful of fresh basil leaves, **torn or shredded**

Freshly grated Pecorino Romano **cheese, for garnish**

1 cozy food

2 make your own takeout

3 fancy fake-outs

Years ago I taught an individual beef Wellington recipe on the Food Network and the response was fantastic. I have updated that recipe, page 184, and provided you with many more in the same style—what I call fancy fake-outs. These meals look very impressive and in some cases appear labor intensive but in fact each is very easily prepared and de-licious! Only you need know that you didn't even break a sweat preparing them! Pull these recipes out for affordable solutions on date nights, special occasions, or any night you need to impress for less money and with less time. Dining *in* rather than out becomes a bigger bargain the pricier the ingredients. Forget the cake. Have your *steak* and eat it, too!

turkey cutlets with sausage & zucchini & tipsy gravy

SERVES 4

1½ pounds turkey breast cutlets

Salt and pepper

1 teaspoon poultry seasoning

1 cup plus 3 tablespoons all-purpose flour

2 large eggs, lightly beaten

1 cup bread crumbs

½ cup cornmeal

½ cup grated Parmigiano-Reggiano **cheese**

Zest of 1 orange

2 sprigs of fresh rosemary, **leaves removed and finely chopped**

Olive oil or vegetable oil for shallow frying

¾ pound sweet Italian sausage **(bulk or 3 short links cut from casing)**

1 medium onion, **chopped**

1 red bell pepper, **seeded and chopped**

2 large garlic cloves, **chopped**

2 small to medium zucchini, **cut into bite-size chunks**

2 tablespoons chopped fresh thyme leaves

3 tablespoons butter

1 cup pinot noir wine

2 cups turkey or chicken stock

Season the turkey cutlets with salt, pepper, and the poultry seasoning. Set up dishes with the 1 cup of flour, the beaten eggs, and, in a third dish, the bread crumbs combined with the cornmeal, cheese, orange zest, and rosemary. Coat the cutlets in the flour, egg, then the bread-crumb mixture. Heat ¼ inch of oil in a large skillet for shallow frying of the turkey over medium to medium-high heat. ■ While the oil heats up, heat a drizzle of oil in another skillet over medium-high heat. Add the sausage to the second skillet and cook until brown, about 5 minutes, stirring occasionally to break up lumps. Add the onions, bell pepper, garlic, zucchini, thyme, and salt and pepper. Cover and cook for 10 to 12 minutes, until the zucchini is tender. ■ Cook the cutlets for 4 minutes on each side to deep golden. Cook them in batches and set the prepared cutlets on a baking rack to keep crisp. ■ Melt the butter in a small skillet over medium to medium-high heat. Whisk in the 3 tablespoons of flour, cook for 1 minute, add the wine, and reduce for about a minute. Whisk in the stock, cook to thicken for 3 to 4 minutes, and season with salt and pepper. ■ Mound the sausage and vegetable mixture on plates, top with the cutlets, then douse with gravy and serve.

For an any-day Thanksgiving experience, finish this meal with **Easiest-Ever Baked Stuffed Apples** (page 302) with **ice cream**.

Serve with a green salad or try with **Spinach Salad with Slumped Mushrooms** (page 268).

quick fake-out
stuffed eggplant

Preheat the oven to 475°F. ■ Halve 4 of the eggplants lengthwise. Pour about 4 tablespoons of EVOO on a rimmed baking sheet. Season the cut eggplant with salt and pepper and place cut side down into the EVOO. Place in the oven and roast for 20 minutes or until tender. ■ Cut the remaining eggplant into ½-inch dice. Brown the beef or lamb over medium-high heat in the remaining 1 tablespoon of EVOO, add the tomato paste, onions, garlic, diced eggplant, and raisins, season with salt and pepper, and cook for 8 to 10 minutes to soften the eggplant and onions. Remove from the heat and add the pine nuts and basil. ■ While the meat cooks, melt the butter in a small skillet over medium heat, add the bread crumbs, and toast until golden. Transfer to a bowl and cool. ■ Add the parsley and cheese to the toasted bread crumbs, then add half of this mixture to the meat. ■ Remove the eggplant halves from the oven, flip the pieces over, and transfer to a serving platter. Top each halved eggplant with a mound of stuffing and sprinkle the remaining cheesy bread crumbs over the top to serve.

SERVES 4

5 small firm eggplants, **6 to 7 inches long and 3 inches wide, or 5 large Japanese eggplants of about the same size**

5 tablespoons olive oil **or vegetable oil**

Salt **and** pepper

1 pound ground beef **or lamb**

1 tablespoon tomato paste

1 small to medium onion

3 to 4 garlic cloves, **finely chopped**

A small handful of raisins

3 to 4 tablespoons toasted pine nuts

A handful of fresh basil leaves, **torn or chopped**

3 tablespoons butter

1 cup bread crumbs

½ cup fresh flat-leaf parsley **leaves, a couple generous handfuls, finely chopped**

½ cup finely grated Pecorino Romano **cheese**

chicken cutlets with orange & arugula

1½ **cups** bread crumbs

½ **cup grated** Parmigiano-Reggiano cheese

Freshly grated nutmeg

A handful of fresh flat-leaf parsley **leaves, finely chopped**

Zest of 1 orange

1 cup all-purpose flour

3 eggs, **beaten**

4 small boneless skinless chicken breast **halves, about 6 ounces each**

Salt and pepper

Olive oil **or vegetable oil, for frying**

2 seedless oranges

2 yellow or orange tomatoes, **seeded and diced**

1 sprig of fresh oregano, **leaves removed and finely chopped (optional)**

½ **small** red onion **or 2 to 3 scallions, chopped**

2 tablespoons EVOO **(extra-virgin olive oil)**

4 cups baby arugula leaves

Combine the bread crumbs, cheese, nutmeg, parsley, and orange zest in a shallow bowl. Place the flour in a second dish and the eggs in a third, positioned between the flour and the bread crumbs. ■ Cut into the chicken and across horizontally to butterfly each piece open. Lightly pound the chicken between wax papper, parchment paper, or plastic wrap into 4 large, very thin cutlets. Season the cutlets with salt and pepper and coat them with the flour, eggs, and bread-crumb mixture. Heat ½ inch of frying oil in a very large skillet over medium to medium-high heat. When the oil is hot, cook the cutlets 1 or 2 at a time, depending on the pan size, for about 2 minutes per side. As the cutlets are done, place on a baking rack to drain. The cutlets may be served at room temperature but you want them to remain crisp. ■ While the cutlets cook, peel and section the oranges and dice. Combine with the tomatoes, oregano, onion, EVOO, and salt and pepper to taste. When ready to serve, gently mix in the arugula leaves. ■ Top the cutlets with mounds of orange and arugula salad and serve.

John and
I eat this cozy
supper all the time.
When we have company,
we start with or serve
as a side **Milanese
Fettuccine Alfredo**
(page 267).

gazpacho pasta

Preheat the oven to 425°F and bring a large pot of water to a boil over high heat. Salt the water and cook the pasta to al dente. Heads up: Reserve a cup of starchy cooking water just before draining. ■ Scatter the tomatoes and zucchini onto a rimmed baking sheet and drizzle them with about 2 tablespoons of EVOO and some salt and pepper. Roast in the oven until the tomatoes have burst and the zucchini is tender, about 20 minutes. ■ Meanwhile, to a food processor add the celery, parsley, cilantro, almonds, garlic, and lime zest and juice. Turn on the food processor and stream in EVOO, about ¼ to ⅓ cup. A splash of water or vegetable stock can help the pesto move in the processor. ■ Toss together in a large bowl the pasta, pesto, reserved cooking water, pimientos or roasted peppers, and roasted tomatoes and zucchini. Season with hot sauce and toss to combine. Garnish with scallions and grated cheese. ■

SERVES 4 TO 6

Salt

1 pound penne pasta **or whole-wheat penne pasta**

2 pints grape tomatoes

2 medium zucchini, **chopped into ¼-inch dice**

¼ to ⅓ cup plus 2 tablespoons EVOO (extra-virgin olive oil), divided

Black pepper

3 to 4 celery stalks **from the heart, finely chopped**

1 cup fresh flat-leaf parsley **leaves, two large handfuls, chopped**

¼ cup fresh cilantro **leaves, a small handful, chopped**

½ cup sliced almonds, **toasted**

1 garlic clove, **minced**

Zest and juice of 1 lime

2 to 3 pimientos **or roasted red peppers, chopped**

A few dashes of hot sauce

Sliced scallions, **for garnish**

Grated manchego cheese **or Pecorino Romano cheese, for topping**

florentine prosciutto-wrapped chicken

SERVES 4 TO 6

1 (10-ounce) box frozen spinach, defrosted

3 tablespoons pine nuts

½ cup ricotta cheese

¼ cup grated Parmigiano-Reggiano cheese

2 garlic cloves, grated or finely chopped

Salt and pepper

Freshly grated nutmeg

6 chicken breasts

6 slices (⅓ pound) Prosciutto di Parma

3 to 4 tablespoons EVOO (extra-virgin olive oil)

Preheat the oven to 400°F. ■ Wring out the defrosted spinach in a clean kitchen towel. ■ Lightly toast the pine nuts in a small dry skillet over medium heat. Watch them so they don't burn. Combine the nuts with the spinach in a bowl. Mix in the cheeses, garlic, salt, pepper, and nutmeg. ■ Cut into and across—but not all the way through—the chicken breasts with a sharp knife, opening them up like a book. Season the chicken with salt and pepper. Fill each with a small mound of spinach stuffing. Fold the chicken breasts back over the stuffing and wrap each breast with prosciutto to seal them up, being careful to cover the whole breast. Brush the chicken all over with some EVOO and roast on a rimmed baking sheet for 18 to 20 minutes, until cooked through.

chicken cutlets brasciole

Pour the very hot water in a small bowl. Add the raisins and plump for 5 minutes. ■ Lightly toast the pine nuts in a small dry skillet over medium-low heat. Watch them so they don't burn. Set them aside on a plate to cool. ■ Place the parsley, lemon zest, garlic, bread, cheese, raisins, and nuts into a processor and pulse into a stuffing. ■ Butterfly the chicken by cutting into and across the breast but not all the way through, so that it opens like a book. Pound out the cutlets and season the chicken with salt and pepper. Fill the breasts with stuffing, then roll and secure with toothpicks. ■ Heat the EVOO and butter in a large skillet over medium-high heat. Brown the chicken all over for 7 to 8 minutes, then remove from the pan and deglaze the pan with the wine. Scrape up the drippings, stir in the tomato sauce and tarragon, and return the chicken to the sauce. Cover and simmer for 15 minutes, or until cooked through, then slice and serve.

SERVES 4

½ cup very hot tap water

A handful of golden raisins

¼ cup pine nuts

1 cup fresh flat-leaf parsley leaves

1 tablespoon grated lemon zest

2 garlic cloves, finely chopped

3 slices white sandwich bread, torn into pieces

½ cup grated Parmigiano-Reggiano cheese

4 pieces of boneless, skinless chicken breast

Salt and pepper

2 tablespoons EVOO (extra-virgin olive oil)

2 tablespoons butter

1 cup dry white wine

2 cups tomato sauce

2 tablespoons fresh tarragon leaves, from a few sprigs, chopped

crispy parm-crusted
fillet of fish & buttery bow
ties with peas

Salt

1 pound bow-tie pasta

1 cup all-purpose flour

2 tablespoons Old Bay seafood seasoning

2 large eggs

1 cup plain, fine bread crumbs **or cracker crumbs**

1½ cups grated Parmigiano-Reggiano **cheese**

2 tablespoons fresh thyme **leaves, finely chopped**

2 lemons

4 (6-ounce) fillets of tilapia **or sole**

7 tablespoons EVOO **(extra-virgin olive oil)**

1 medium onion, **finely chopped**

2 to 3 large garlic cloves, **finely chopped or grated**

1 cup frozen peas, **defrosted**

3 tablespoons butter

¼ cup fresh mint leaves, **finely chopped**

¼ cup fresh flat-leaf parsley **leaves, finely chopped**

Black pepper

Preheat the oven to 250°F. Arrange a cooling rack atop a rimmed baking sheet. ■ Bring a large pot of water to a boil for the pasta. Salt the water and cook the pasta to al dente. Heads up: You need to reserve a ladle of starchy cooking water for the pasta and peas just before draining. ■ While the water comes to a boil, set up three dishes for breading the fillets. In the first, combine the flour with the Old Bay. In the second, beat the eggs with a splash of water. In the third, combine the bread crumbs, ½ cup of the Parmigiano, the thyme, and the grated zest of 1 lemon. Dip the fish fillets in the flour, then in the egg, and finally in the bread-crumb mixture. ■ While the pasta is cooking, heat a large skillet over medium to medium-high heat with 4 tablespoons of the EVOO. Sauté 2 fillets at a time for 6 to 7 minutes until golden, turning once. Place the first batch on a cooling rack atop the baking sheet to keep crisp. You'll need to add 2 tablespoons more EVOO to the pan for the next batch and let the oil get hot again before cooking the second batch. ■ While the fish cooks, heat the remaining tablespoon of EVOO in a skillet over medium heat. Add the onions and garlic and cook until tender, 5 to 6 minutes. Add the peas and butter to the skillet with the onions and garlic and heat the peas through. Add the reserved ladle of starchy cooking water and the drained pasta. Turn off the heat, toss with the mint, parsley, and a couple handfuls of cheese, then season with salt and pepper. ■ Serve the fish alongside the pasta. Cut the lemons into wedges and serve for topping fish.

Serve with a simple salad; or, to entertain with this meal, try serving with **Chunky Puttanesca Crostini** (page 270) and **Black Pepper–Cinnamon Honey with Fruit and Ice Cream** (page 304).

butter-me-up bucatini
with scallops

Bring a large pot of water to a boil for the pasta, salt the water, and cook the pasta to just shy of al dente, reserving 1 cup cooking liquid just before draining. ■ Toss the scallops with the Old Bay and 1 sliced lemon, then set aside for a few minutes. ■ Over low heat, start to melt the butter in a small pot, then stir in the garlic and red pepper flakes and let bubble gently for 10 minutes. Finely chop the parsley and reserve. ■ Heat a large skillet with the EVOO over medium-high heat. Add the scallops, sliced lemon, and fennel seed and cook for 5 to 6 minutes, turning once, until the scallops become opaque and are just cooked through. Add the white wine or vermouth and the juice of the remaining lemon and transfer to a bowl. ■ Stir the parsley into the garlic butter. ■ Add the pasta, reserved cooking water, scallops, and garlic butter to a pasta bowl and toss for 1 to 2 minutes until the liquids are absorbed by the pasta. Adjust the seasoning to taste.

SERVES 4

Salt

1 pound bucatini pasta

1½ pounds large sea scallops, **muscle removed, patted dry or** shrimp, **peeled and deveined**

1 tablespoon Old Bay seafood seasoning

2 lemons

8 tablespoons (1 stick) butter

6 garlic cloves, **finely chopped**

1 teaspoon crushed red pepper flakes

1 cup loosely packed fresh flat-leaf parsley **leaves**

2 tablespoons EVOO (extra-virgin olive oil)

1 teaspoon fennel seed

½ cup white wine **or white vermouth**

chili-lime fish fry with
tex-mex peperonata

SERVES 4

PEPERONATA

2 tablespoons EVOO **(extra-virgin olive oil)**

1 red onion**, thinly sliced**

2 garlic cloves**, finely chopped**

2 jalapeño peppers**, seeded and thinly sliced**

1 red bell pepper**, seeded and thinly sliced**

1 green bell pepper**, seeded and thinly sliced**

Salt **and pepper**

2 tablespoons tomato paste

1 cup beer **or chicken stock**

A handful of fresh cilantro **leaves, chopped**

CHILI-LIME FISH FRY

4 tilapia **fillets**

Salt **and pepper**

1 cup all-purpose flour

2 eggs

1 cup bread crumbs

2 limes

2 tablespoons chili powder**, a couple palmfuls**

2 teaspoons garlic powder**, ⅔ palmful**

2 teaspoons onion powder**, ⅔ palmful**

2 tablespoons chopped fresh thyme **leaves or 2 teaspoons dried thyme**

¼ cup vegetable, canola, or safflower oil

To prepare the peperonata, heat the EVOO in a skillet over medium-high heat. Add the onions, garlic, jalapeño and bell peppers, and salt and pepper. Sauté until the peppers are crisp-tender, 5 to 6 minutes. Stir in the tomato paste, cook for 2 minutes, then add the beer or stock and stir for a minute or two more. Top with the cilantro and set aside. ■ Season the fish with salt and pepper. Arrange 3 shallow dishes; place the flour in one, beat the eggs in the second, and scatter the bread crumbs in the third. Season the bread crumbs with 1 tablespoon grated lime zest, the chili powder, garlic powder, onion powder, and thyme. Coat the fish in the flour, eggs, and seasoned bread crumbs. ■ Meanwhile, heat the oil in a large skillet over medium to medium-high heat. If the pan is not large enough to fry 4 fillets, heat the oven to 275°F and place a cooling rack on a rimmed baking sheet. As you fry the fish, transfer it to the rack in the hot oven to keep warm. Cook the fish for 3 to 4 minutes on each side, or until deeply golden and crispy. Season with a little extra salt and top the fish with lots of lime juice and then the peperonata.

Serve with rice prepared according to the package directions or check out **Corny Polenta** (page 270).

wild mushroom broken spaghetti "risotto"
with arugula & hazelnuts

Heat a medium sauté pan or risotto pan with the 3 tablespoons of EVOO over medium to medium-high heat. Add the onions and garlic to the pan, season with salt and pepper to taste, and sauté until tender, 4 to 5 minutes. ■ Place the mushrooms, stock, and 2 cups water in a sauce pot and heat. Keep warm on low. Add the pasta to the sauté pan and toast until it is deeply golden in color and very nutty in fragrance, 6 to 7 minutes. Stir in the wine and let it cook away for 1 minute. Ladle in warm stock every few minutes, stirring for a good minute with each addition of stock to develop starches. Evaporate almost all of the liquid before each addition of stock. The pasta will cook up more quickly than rice, so start tasting after 8 or 9 minutes of cooking time once you begin to add stock. When you are down to the last cup of liquids, remove the mushrooms, chop, and add to the pasta. ■ While the pasta cooks, toast the hazelnuts on medium-low heat in a dry skillet until fragrant, 3 to 5 minutes. Peel the nuts by rubbing the skins off in a clean kitchen towel. ■ When the pasta is cooked to al dente, add the butter and cheese to the pan, then stir. ■ Dress the arugula with lemon juice, a drizzle of EVOO, and salt and pepper to taste. ■ Serve the pasta in shallow bowls topped with arugula and hazelnuts.

SERVES 4

3 tablespoons EVOO (extra-virgin olive oil), plus a drizzle

1 medium onion, finely chopped

2 large garlic cloves, grated or finely chopped

Salt and pepper

1 (1-ounce) package dried mixed wild mushrooms or porcini mushrooms

1 quart chicken stock

1 pound spaghetti, broken into small pieces

½ cup dry white wine

¾ cup hazelnuts

2 tablespoons butter

¾ cup Parmigiano-Reggiano cheese, a few handfuls

4 cups arugula

½ lemon, juiced

super scampi

SERVES 6

3 tablespoons EVOO (extra-virgin olive oil)

6 anchovies

6 garlic cloves, chopped

1 teaspoon crushed red pepper flakes

1 cup dry white wine

2 stems of fresh oregano, leaves stripped and finely chopped

A generous handful of fresh flat-leaf parsley leaves, finely chopped

3 tablespoons butter, cut into small pieces

1 quart chicken stock

1 pound linguine

2½ pounds large shrimp, peeled and deveined

Zest and juice of 1 lemon

1 cup fresh basil leaves, about 20, torn

Salt and pepper

Crusty bread, torn into pieces

Heat the EVOO over medium heat in a large skillet. Add the anchovies, garlic, and pepper flakes to the pan and cook until the anchovies melt into the oil, a couple of minutes. Add the wine, oregano, and parsley to the pan and reduce the wine for 1 minute, then melt the butter into the sauce. Add the stock and 2 cups water to the pan and bring to a boil. Stir the pasta and shrimp into the pan and reduce the heat. Simmer for 7 to 8 minutes until the pasta is al dente and the shrimp are firm. Stir in the lemon zest and juice and the basil and season with salt and pepper to taste. Serve directly from the hot pan with fresh crusty bread.

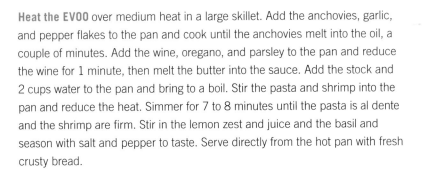

Serve with salad or a dark green vegetable and crusty bread for mopping.

pork chops pizzaiola

Season the chops with salt and pepper. Heat the EVOO in a large skillet over medium-high heat. Throw in the crushed garlic, flip it around, then add the chops and cook until golden brown and caramelized, 2 to 3 minutes per side. Transfer the chops to a plate and reserve. Add the fennel seed, onions, red pepper flakes, and oregano to the pan and reduce the heat a bit. Cook until the onions are tender, 7 to 8 minutes, then add the tomato paste and stir for 1 minute. Add the wine, stir for a minute more, then add the stock and stir to combine. Slide the chops back into the pan and simmer for 5 or 6 minutes to finish cooking the meat through.

SERVES 4

4 (1½-inch-thick) bone-in pork chops

Salt and pepper

2 tablespoons EVOO (extra-virgin olive oil)

1 large garlic clove, crushed

1 teaspoon fennel seed

1 medium onion, sliced

1 teaspoon crushed red pepper flakes

2 sprigs of fresh oregano, leaves stripped, or 1 teaspoon dried oregano

¼ cup tomato paste

1 cup red wine

2 cups chicken stock

lemon garlic sirloin tips &
rice pilaf with arugula

2 pounds sirloin tips, **trimmed and cut into bite-size cubes**

4 tablespoons EVOO (extra-virgin olive oil)

⅓ cup orzo pasta

1 cup white rice

2 cups chicken stock

2 cups arugula, **chopped**

2 handfuls grated Parmigiano-Reggiano **cheese**

Salt **and** pepper

4 large garlic cloves, **finely chopped**

½ cup fresh flat-leaf parsley, **a couple handfuls, finely chopped**

1 lemon

½ cup white vermouth **or dry white wine**

Bring the meat to room temperature. ■ Heat about 1 tablespoon of the EVOO in a sauce pot over medium heat. Add the orzo and toast until deeply golden, 4 to 5 minutes. Add the white rice and toss with the orzo. Add the stock to the pot and bring to a boil. Reduce the heat to a simmer, cover, and cook for 16 to 17 minutes, until the orzo and rice are tender. Add the arugula and cheese and toss to combine. ■ While the pilaf is simmering, pat the beef dry. Heat the remaining 3 tablespoons of EVOO in a large, heavy skillet or cast-iron skillet over medium-high to high heat. When the oil smokes, add the meat and brown before turning. When the meat is evenly browned all over, after about 5 minutes, season it liberally with salt and pepper. Toss the meat for 2 minutes, then add the garlic, parsley, and a little lemon zest. Toss the meat around for a minute. Add the white vermouth and juice of the lemon to the pan and deglaze. Turn off the heat and toss. Place meat alongside the rice pilaf and serve immediately.

Serve with a **tomato salad** or try **Red White Beans** (page 271).

Serve with a simple cucumber or tomato salad or try the **Lentil–Potato Salad** (page 271).

crispy curry fried chicken

In a small bowl, mix together the curry, chili powder, onion and garlic powders, poultry seasoning, celery seed or ground cardamom, and lime zest, and set aside. ■ Combine half of the spice mixture with the yogurt. Season the chicken with salt and pepper. Coat the chicken with the yogurt. This can be done as much as 24 hours ahead. Keep the chicken, covered, in the refrigerator until about 30 minutes before you are ready to cook it. ■ Place the flour in a large brown paper sack, add the remainder of the spice mix to it, and shake the bag. Add 4 chicken pieces and shake to coat. ■ In a large pot at least five inches high, heat 2½ to 3 inches of frying oil over medium to medium-high heat. Insert the handle of a wooden spoon in the oil. If rapid bubbles come out and away from the handle, the oil is ready. Fry the 4 pieces of coated chicken for 12 minutes, turning once. Coat the remaining chicken while the first batch fries up. Cool the chicken on a rack and sprinkle with a little extra salt. Allow the oil to heat back up for a minute or two, then fry the second batch. Serve with the lime wedges to squirt over the crispy curry chicken.

SERVES 4

2 tablespoons curry powder, such as Madras

1 tablespoon chili powder

1 tablespoon onion powder

1 tablespoon garlic powder

1 tablespoon poultry seasoning

1 teaspoon celery seed or ground cardamom

1 tablespoon grated lime zest plus 8 wedges of lime

1 cup whole-fat plain yogurt

1 whole chicken, cut for frying into 8 pieces

Salt and pepper

2 cups all-purpose flour

Vegetable, safflower, or peanut oil, for frying

NOTE Quadruple the spice mix recipe and store it for up to 6 months in an airtight container.

I call this **Almost Tandoori Chicken.** You do not need an actual tandoor oven, but it tastes pretty close to the real deal.

almost tandoori chicken

Preheat the oven to 500°F. ■ Combine the yogurt with the zest of the lime and the spices. ■ Cut the chicken into large chunks. Season the chicken liberally with salt and pepper, then add to the yogurt and coat evenly. Place a wire rack on a rimmed baking sheet or use a slotted broiler pan for cooking. Arrange the chicken on the rack or slotted pan and roast for 15 minutes, or until it's charred at the edges and the juices run clear. ■ Combine the apple, tomatoes, and scallions, and dress with the juice of the lime, the oil, and salt and pepper. ■ Serve the chicken with the apple-tomato topping and warm bread.

SERVES 4

1 cup Greek yogurt

1 lime

1 tablespoon ground turmeric, a palmful

1 tablespoon ground coriander

1 tablespoon smoked paprika

½ tablespoon ground cumin, ½ palmful

1 teaspoon ground cardamom, ⅓ palmful

2 pounds boneless skinless chicken thighs

Salt and pepper

1 green apple, peeled and thinly sliced into matchsticks

2 plum tomatoes, seeded and very thinly sliced lengthwise

4 scallions, thinly sliced

2 tablespoons olive or vegetable oil

4 pieces store-bought naan bread, plain or flavored, warmed

zin-zen chicken

SERVES 4

1 cup **white or light brown** rice

2 cups chicken stock

Zest and juice of 1 orange, **divided**

3 tablespoons EVOO **(extra-virgin olive oil)**

2 pounds boneless skinless chicken breasts, **cut into bite-size chunks**

Salt **and** pepper

1 red bell pepper, **seeded and cut into bite-size pieces**

1 green bell pepper, **seeded and cut into bite-size pieces**

2 garlic cloves, **finely chopped or grated**

1 inch of fresh gingerroot, **peeled and grated, or 1 teaspoon ground ginger**

1 red onion, **cut into bite-size pieces**

1 tablespoon butter

1 tablespoon all-purpose flour

1 cup Zinfandel wine

3 tablespoons tamari **(aged soy sauce)**

2 teaspoons Chinese five-spice powder

4 scallions, **sliced on the bias**

In a medium pot over medium-high heat, combine the rice, chicken stock, orange zest, and about 1 tablespoon EVOO. Bring the liquid up to a bubble and then reduce the heat to low, then cover the pot. Simmer the rice until it has absorbed all of the liquid, about 20 minutes. ■ While the rice is cooking, place a large skillet over medium-high heat with the remaining 2 tablespoons of EVOO. Season the chicken with salt and pepper, and sauté until golden brown and cooked through, 7 to 8 minutes. Remove the chicken from the skillet and reserve on a plate. ■ Return the skillet to medium-high heat and add the red and green peppers, garlic, ginger, and onion to the pan. Sauté for 4 to 5 minutes, until the vegetables are tender. Season the veggies with salt and pepper, and push everything over to one side of the pan. Add the butter to the pan, and as it is melting, sprinkle the flour over it; cook for about 30 seconds. Add the wine, tamari, and five-spice powder and stir to combine. Return the chicken to the pan and simmer until the sauce is thickened and the chicken is heated through, 2 to 3 minutes more. ■ Fluff the rice with a fork and stir in the scallions and orange juice. Serve the stir-fry over the rice.

Serve with white or brown rice or couscous. Check out the **Pine Nut–Saffron Pilaf** (page 272).

moroccan
lemon-olive chicken

Slice 1 lemon into ½-inch-thick rounds. ■ Heat the EVOO in a skillet over medium-high heat. When the oil ripples and begins to smoke, add the chicken pieces, season with salt and pepper, and brown for 3 to 4 minutes. Add the onions, garlic, lemon rounds, and bay leaves. Cook, stirring frequently, for 6 to 7 more minutes. Add the spices, stock, and olives to the skillet and cook for 5 minutes to reduce the liquid. Remove from the heat, discard the bay leaves, squeeze the juice from the remaining lemon into the skillet, and stir in the mint and parsley. Discard the cinnamon stick. Serve with rice or couscous.

SERVES 4

2 lemons **or Meyer lemons**

2 tablespoons EVOO **(extra-virgin olive oil)**

2 pounds boneless skinless chicken thighs, **trimmed and cut into large bite-size pieces**

Salt **and** pepper

1 large onion, **thinly sliced**

4 large garlic cloves, **crushed**

2 fresh bay leaves

2 teaspoons ground turmeric, **⅔ palmful**

2 teaspoons ground coriander, **⅔ palmful**

2 teaspoons ground cumin, **⅔ palmful**

1 cinnamon stick

2 cups chicken stock

1 cup large pitted green olives

A handful of fresh mint leaves, **finely chopped**

2 handfuls of fresh flat-leaf parsley leaves, **finely chopped**

margarita fish tacos

SERVES 4

2 ounces tequila

Zest and juice of 1 lime

3 tablespoons vegetable oil

1 tablespoon Old Bay seafood seasoning

1 teaspoon chili powder

4 (6- to 8-ounce) mahimahi or halibut fillets

1 small to medium red onion, chopped

2 garlic cloves, finely chopped

8 to 10 tomatillos, peeled and coarsely chopped

1 teaspoon ground cumin

1 jalapeño pepper, seeded and chopped

Salt and pepper

1 small ripe avocado

Zest and juice of 1 lemon

1 generous tablespoon honey

Cooking spray

8 soft flour tortillas

½ small white or red cabbage, shredded

Combine the tequila with the lime zest and juice, 2 tablespoons of the oil, the Old Bay seasoning, and the chili powder. Coat the fish in the dressing and heat a grill pan or outdoor grill. ■ While the grill heats, add the remaining tablespoon of oil to a skillet over medium-high heat. Cook the onions and garlic for 2 to 3 minutes to begin to soften, then add the chopped tomatillos, cumin, and jalapeños. Season with salt and pepper, and cook to soften, 6 to 7 minutes more. Put the tomatillo mixture in the food processor with the flesh of the avocado, lemon juice and zest, and honey. Process until a thick salsa forms. Transfer to a bowl. ■ Spray the grill with cooking spray and cook the fish for 3 to 4 minutes on each side. Place the soft tortillas over an open flame on a stove burner or grill to soften and char. ■ Wrap the fish, cabbage, and salsa inside the tortillas and serve.

This meal can be enjoyed for breakfast, lunch, or dinner. For an added sweet treat or a special Sunday brunch, add **Berries with Almond Cream and Amaretti** (page 304).

rosemary potato frittata &
tomato-mozzarella crostini

Preheat the oven to 450°F. ■ Heat 3 tablespoons of the EVOO in a medium ovenproof skillet over medium-low heat with the crushed garlic. Let the garlic infuse the oil while you thinly slice the potatoes and onion, then remove the garlic. Add the potatoes and onions to the pan, season with rosemary, salt, and pepper, and raise the heat a little. Cook the potatoes and onions for 6 to 7 minutes, then turn and cook for 5 more minutes. ■ Meanwhile, in a large bowl, beat the eggs with the milk or cream. When the potatoes are just tender, pour the egg mixture evenly around and under the potatoes. Transfer the skillet to the oven and bake for 10 to 12 minutes, until golden on top. Scatter the cheese on top, turn off the oven, and let the frittata stand in the oven for a couple more minutes. ■ While the frittata cooks, prepare the crostini. Arrange the bread on a rimmed baking sheet and place in the oven to toast while the frittata cooks. ■ Halve the bocconcini and place them in a bowl, then finely dice the prosciutto, halve the tomatoes, and add both with the parsley to the bowl with the cheese. Add the scallions, basil, and dress the salad with a liberal dose of EVOO, salt, and pepper. Remove the toasts from the oven. Top the toasts with the tomato-mozzarella salad and serve alongside wedges of the frittata.

SERVES 4

6 tablespoons EVOO (extra-virgin olive oil)

1 large garlic clove, **crushed**

1 pound baby potatoes

1 small onion

3 to 4 sprigs of fresh rosemary, **leaves removed and finely chopped**

Salt **and** pepper

12 eggs, **beaten**

½ cup milk, **half-and-half, or cream**

½ cup grated Parmigiano-Reggiano **cheese**

8 slices peasant bread

1 pint bocconcini **(small bites of fresh mozzarella in water)**

1 (¼-inch-thick) slice prosciutto

1 pint multicolored baby or grape tomatoes **or red grape tomatoes**

A handful of fresh flat-leaf parsley **leaves, finely chopped**

4 thin scallions, **whites and greens, trimmed and thinly sliced**

A handful of fresh basil **leaves, thinly sliced**

fondue with apple brandy

SERVES 6

1¾ cups dry white wine

1 tablespoon lemon juice

¾ pound Gruyère cheese, shredded

¾ pound Emmentaler cheese, shredded

1½ tablespoons cornstarch

⅓ cup apple brandy

Freshly grated nutmeg

1 to 2 pinches of cayenne pepper

Place the wine in a fondue pot and bring to a bubble over medium heat. Reduce the heat to a simmer, add the lemon juice, then add the cheeses in handfuls, stirring in a figure-eight motion with a wooden spoon. When the cheese is fully melted, stir the cornstarch into the brandy until smooth, then add to the cheese. Season with nutmeg and cayenne pepper to taste and serve in the fondue pot over a warming station.

Fondue should be called fun-due because it's easy to make and fun to eat with a gathering of family or friends.

Serve with any vegetables, sausages, meats, or breads for dipping. I have suggested some dippers, or you can freestyle.

fondue dippers:
bacon-wrapped chicken with spinach, blanched vegetables

Preheat the oven to 400°F. ■ Defrost the spinach in the microwave. ■ Drizzle a little EVOO on a large plate. Halve the bacon across and reserve. Halve the chicken tenders and slide them onto the plate with the EVOO, then toss with salt, pepper, and the poultry seasoning. Wring out the spinach in a clean dish towel and separate the spinach in a small dish. Top each piece of chicken with a little spinach and wrap with bacon, then place seam side down on a rimmed baking sheet. Bake for 18 to 20 minutes, until golden and firm. ■ Meanwhile, bring a few inches of water to a boil. Have a large bowl of ice water ready for shocking the veggies. Add salt to the water. Blanch the radishes for 1 minute, then shock them in the ice water, drain, and reserve. Do the same with the bell pepper sticks; fish them out with tongs, a small strainer, or a "spider" mesh ladle. Add the asparagus and cook for 2 to 3 minutes until tender-crisp, then shock and reserve. ■ Arrange the chicken, vegetables, onions, cornichons, and pretzels around the fondue pot and serve with the cubed bread.

SERVES 6

1 (10-ounce) box frozen chopped spinach

EVOO (extra-virgin olive oil), for drizzling

6 slices smoky bacon

12 chicken tenders

Salt and pepper

1 teaspoon poultry seasoning

1 bunch of radishes, trimmed

1 large red bell pepper, seeded and sliced into ½-inch-thick sticks

1 bundle of white or thin green asparagus, trimmed

1 jar pickled pearl onions, drained

1 jar cornichons or mini gherkins, drained

1 bag pretzel rods

1 baguette, cubed for dipping

My mom is from Sicily, where Marsala is made. This is a simple recipe for you to share with your loved ones.

pork tenderloin medallions
with marsala sauce & pasta

Bring a large pot of water to a boil for the pasta. When the water boils, add salt and cook the pasta to al dente. Drain the pasta. ■ While the water comes to a boil, slice each of the pork tenderloins into 2-inch pieces. Arrange the meat in batches between parchment paper and pound it into thin medallions, ⅛ inch thick. Season the meat with salt and pepper and dredge in the ½ cup flour to coat lightly. ■ Heat a tablespoon or two of the EVOO at a time in a large skillet over medium-high heat and brown the medallions in batches for 2 to 3 minutes on each side. Keep the cooked meat on a platter. ■ When the pork is finished cooking, add the butter to the skillet. Then add the mushrooms to the skillet and cook until golden brown, 7 to 8 minutes, adding the garlic to the pan after 3 to 4 minutes. Season the mushrooms with salt and pepper. Sprinkle the mushrooms with the 2 tablespoons flour and cook for 1 more minute. Add the Marsala to the pan and cook for a minute or so, until the wine is reduced by about half. Add the chicken stock to the pan and bring the sauce up to a bubble. Slide the meat back in and stir in the parsley. ■ Remove the pork and arrange on a platter or dinner plates. Toss the cooked pasta with the remaining sauce and serve alongside.

SERVES 4

Salt

1 pound pappardelle **or fettuccine**

2 pork tenderloins**, 1½ to 1¾ pounds total, trimmed of connective tissue and silver skin (you can ask your butcher to do this)**

Black pepper

½ cup plus 2 tablespoons all-purpose flour

5 tablespoons EVOO **(extra-virgin olive oil)**

4 tablespoons (½ stick) butter

1 pound cremini mushrooms, **thinly sliced**

3 to 4 garlic cloves, **finely chopped**

1 cup Marsala

1 cup chicken stock

½ cup fresh flat-leaf parsley **leaves, finely chopped**

blt bacon, leek & tomato
polenta-crusted frittata

SERVES 4

2 tablespoons EVOO (extra-virgin olive oil), divided

2 leeks, cleaned, and whites parts chopped

¼ pound pancetta, cut into small dice

2 garlic cloves, finely chopped or grated

3 cups chicken stock

1 cup quick-cooking polenta

½ cup grated Parmigiano-Reggiano cheese

Black pepper

8 eggs

Salt

2 tablespoons cold butter, cut in pieces

1 pint cherry or grape tomatoes, quartered

2 handfuls of arugula

Juice of 1 lemon

Preheat the oven to 425°F. ■ In a 10-inch ovensafe nonstick skillet, heat 1 tablespoon of the EVOO over medium-high heat and sauté the leeks. Once the leeks are soft, remove and set aside. Reserve the skillet for later. ■ While the leeks are cooking, in a medium sauce pot over medium heat, cook the pancetta until golden brown. Add the garlic and cook for 1 to 2 minutes, until fragrant. Add the stock to the pancetta and garlic, and let it come to a boil. ■ Once the stock is at a boil, add the polenta and stir until thick. Add the cheese and some black pepper to the polenta, then remove from the heat. Pour the polenta into the reserved skillet and lightly press it up the sides and bottom of the skillet, forming a crust that covers the entire pan. Spread the reserved leeks in the bottom of the polenta crust. ■ In a large mixing bowl, whisk together the eggs, salt and pepper, and the pieces of cold butter. Pour the mixture over the leeks in the polenta crust, then transfer to the oven and bake until golden brown and cooked through, about 20 minutes. ■ While the frittata is in the oven, toss the tomatoes, arugula, the remaining tablespoon of EVOO, the lemon juice, salt, and pepper together in a mixing bowl. Once the frittata is golden and firm in the middle, remove from the oven and top with the dressed baby tomatoes and arugula.

chicken suizas
quesadilla cake

Heat a grill pan to medium-high or heat an outdoor grill. ■ Peel, rinse, and halve the tomatillos. Thread them on metal skewers along with the onion quarters, peppers, and garlic. Spray the skewered ingredients with cooking spray and grill for 15 minutes, turning to cook evenly. Preheat the oven to 350°F. Scrape the charred ingredients into a food processor and add the cilantro, lime zest and juice, honey, cumin, and salt. Process to form a sauce; if too thick, add ¼ to ⅓ cup water. Put the chicken in a large bowl and pour the sauce over it, then toss to coat. ■ Char the tortillas on a grill or over a gas burner. Spray a cake pan with cooking spray. Then add a tortilla and top with one quarter of the chicken mixture, 4 rounded teaspoon-size dollops of crème fraîche or sour cream, and some shredded Swiss and Monterey Jack cheese. Add another tortilla and continue to build until you have 4 layers of chicken and cheese and a tortilla on top. Spray the top with cooking spray and place in the hot oven or on an outdoor grill with the lid down to melt the cheese for 5 minutes. Place a plate over the pan and invert the pie. Cut into 4 wedges and serve.

SERVES 4

6 tomatillos

1 medium onion, **peeled and quartered**

1 jalapeño pepper, **seeded and halved**

1 poblano pepper, **seeded and quartered**

2 large garlic cloves, **peeled**

Cooking spray

A small handful of fresh cilantro leaves

Zest and juice of 1 lime

1 tablespoon honey

1 teaspoon ground cumin, **⅓ palmful**

Salt

1 rotisserie chicken, **skin removed and meat shredded**

5 (8-inch) flour tortillas

¾ cup crème fraîche **or sour cream**

2 cups shredded Swiss cheese

2 cups shredded Monterey Jack **or mild cheddar cheese**

sliced steak with watercress, garlic & horseradish baby potatoes

In a large pot, add the potatoes and enough cold water to cover. Bring to a boil, add some salt, and cook until the potatoes are tender, about 15 minutes, then drain. ■ Meanwhile, in a large skillet, add the EVOO and the garlic. Over medium heat, fry the garlic until golden and crisp. Using a slotted spoon, transfer the garlic to a paper towel on a plate to drain. Reserve the skillet with the oil. ■ On a cutting board, slice the steak thin crosswise. Toss with a little flour and the paprika. Heat the reserved oil over medium-high heat. Working in 2 batches, cook the meat until browned all over, 3 to 4 minutes. Transfer to a warm platter. ■ Stir the tomato paste into the skillet over medium-high heat for 30 seconds. Add the wine and scrape the bottom of the pan. ■ Mash the potatoes with the sour cream, milk, horseradish, and most of the chives and season with salt. Sprinkle the remaining chives on top. Pour the sauce over the steak. Top with the watercress and reserved garlic chips. Serve the potatoes alongside the steak.

SERVES 4

2 pounds baby potatoes**, halved**

Salt

¼ cup EVOO **(extra-virgin olive oil)**

3 large garlic cloves**, thinly sliced lengthwise**

1½ pounds sirloin steak**, about 1 inch thick, patted dry**

All-purpose flour**, for coating**

1 teaspoon sweet smoked paprika

1 tablespoon tomato paste

½ cup white wine **(eyeball it)**

½ cup sour cream **or crème fraîche**

3 tablespoons milk **or half-and-half**

2 tablespoons prepared horseradish

¼ cup chopped fresh chives

1 bunch of watercress**, trimmed of root ends**

steaks
topped **with** sweet & spicy salad

SERVES 4

4 flatiron steaks

EVOO (extra-virgin olive oil) for drizzling, plus ¼ cup

Salt **and** pepper

2 tablespoons ketchup

2 tablespoons grainy Dijon mustard

1 tablespoon Worcestershire sauce

1 small garlic clove, **finely chopped**

Juice of 1 lemon

1 large heart of romaine, **chopped**

1 bundle of arugula, **chopped**

Heat a grill pan to high. When the grill is very hot, drizzle the steaks with EVOO and season with salt and pepper. Cook for 3 to 4 minutes on each side for pink centers (a couple minutes longer for medium-well). Rest the meat before serving. ■ Meanwhile, in a salad bowl, combine the ketchup, mustard, Worcestershire sauce, garlic, and lemon juice. Whisk in the ¼ cup EVOO and season with salt and pepper. Add the greens and toss. Serve the salad on top of the steaks.

Serve with **Strawberry-Balsamic Lemonade** (page 305) and **oil and vinegar–dressed slaw** or **Fennel and Pepper Salad** (page 274).

hot sausage burgers
with broccoli rabe

Combine the pork with the red pepper flakes, paprika, fennel, sage, granulated onion, granulated garlic, and salt. Form 4 patties and drizzle with EVOO to coat. ■ Heat a small pot over medium-low heat, add the tomato sauce, brown sugar, Worcestershire, vinegar, and black pepper, then cook for 15 minutes or until thickened to steak-sauce consistency. ■ Bring a couple inches of water to a boil in a medium skillet, salt the water, and cook the broccoli rabe for 5 minutes, then drain. Place the skillet back on the stove and heat the tablespoon of EVOO over medium heat. Add the chopped garlic; chop the broccoli rabe into 2-inch pieces and sauté it in the garlic and oil for 2 minutes. Season with nutmeg to taste. ■ While the water comes to a boil for the broccoli rabe and the tomato sauce reduces, heat a drizzle of EVOO in a skillet over medium-high heat. Add the burgers and cook for 5 to 6 minutes on each side. Melt a slice of provolone over the patties during the last minute of cook time. Tent the pan with foil to help the cheese melt. ■ To serve, pile broccoli rabe on each roll, top with a cheesy sausage patty, and set the top of the roll in place with a slather of warm sauce. Place some chips alongside.

SERVES 4

1¾ to 2 pounds ground pork (ask your butcher for a coarse grind)

1 teaspoon crushed red pepper flakes, ⅓ palmful

2 teaspoons sweet smoked paprika, ⅔ palmful

1½ teaspoons ground fennel or fennel pollen or 1 teaspoon fennel seed

1 teaspoon ground sage, ⅓ palmful

1 teaspoon granulated onion, ⅓ palmful

1 teaspoon granulated garlic, ⅓ palmful

Salt

EVOO (extra-virgin olive oil) for drizzling, plus 1 tablespoon

1 cup tomato sauce

3 tablespoons dark brown sugar

2 tablespoons Worcestershire sauce

1 tablespoon balsamic vinegar

Black pepper

1 small bundle of broccoli rabe, trimmed of tough ends

1 large or 2 small garlic cloves, finely chopped

Freshly grated nutmeg

4 thick deli slices sharp Provolone cheese

4 ciabatta rolls or other crusty rolls, split

Olive oil and rosemary or herb-flavored fancy potato chips, store-bought

saucy skirt steak with orange-spice sweet potatoes

SERVES 4

2½ to 3 pounds skirt steak

2 pounds sweet potatoes, peeled and cut into small chunks

Salt

2 tablespoons butter

1 large sweet onion, very thinly sliced

2 dried ancho peppers, seeded and stemmed

1½ cups chicken stock

1 tablespoon tomato paste

1 tablespoon Worcestershire sauce

EVOO (extra-virgin olive oil) for drizzling, plus 1 tablespoon

Black pepper

2 slices smoky bacon, finely chopped

Zest and juice of 1 orange

1 teaspoon ground coriander, ⅓ palmful

½ teaspoon ground cumin, ⅓ palmful

¼ teaspoon ground cinnamon

A few dashes of hot sauce

Heat a grill pan or grill to high. Place the steaks on the countertop to take off the chill. ■ Place the peeled and cut potatoes in a pot, cover with water, and bring to a boil. Salt the water and cook the potatoes until tender, 15 to 18 minutes. ■ Heat a medium skillet over medium heat, add the butter, melt, then add the onions. Cook, stirring occasionally, until they are caramel in color, about 20 minutes. ■ Place the anchos in a small sauce pot with 1 cup of the stock and add water to cover. Bring to a boil, stir in the tomato paste, reduce the heat to a simmer, and reduce the liquid by half. ■ When the achos and onions are ready, place them with the liquid in a food processor with the Worcestershire sauce. Turn on the processor and stream in a healthy drizzle of EVOO, then season with salt and pepper to taste. ■ Season the meat with salt and pepper, drizzle with EVOO, and grill over high heat for 5 to 6 minutes total, turning once, for rare. Let the meat rest, covered with foil, for 5 minutes or more, until the potatoes are finished. ■ When the sweet potatoes are tender, drain them and return the pot to the stove. Heat 1 tablespoon of oil in the pot over medium heat, cook the bacon until it begins to crisp, then add the orange zest and juice and the potatoes. Mash to the desired consistency, adding up to ½ cup of chicken stock to thin the potatoes as necessary. Season the potatoes with the coriander, cumin, cinnamon, and hot sauce and remove from the heat. ■ Thinly slice the steak. Divide it among 4 plates and pour lots of the steak sauce over the top. Arrange the potatoes alongside and serve.

Serve with wilted spinach, a green salad, or **Garlicky Creamed Corn and Spinach** (page 274).

What's better than **big roasted meatballs** wrapped around **fresh mozzarella cheese**? It's almost too much to wrap your head around.

bocconcini stuffed meatballs
with tomato-pesto sauce

Preheat the oven to 425°F. ■ Place the torn bread in a small bowl, cover with milk, and soak for a few minutes. To a mixing bowl add the ground meats, 2 of the grated or minced garlic cloves, the chopped parsley, a handful of grated cheese, the egg, and salt and pepper. Squeeze the liquid out of the soaked bread and crumble it as you add it to the bowl. Mix to combine. Take a handful of meatball mix in your palm and flatten it, nestle a mozzarella bite into the center, and roll the meat around it, making 16 meatballs total, each about 2 to 3 ounces. Transfer the stuffed meatballs to a rimmed baking sheet as you roll them. Coat the balls in about 2 tablespoons of EVOO and roast for 18 to 20 minutes until they are firm and browned. ■ About 10 minutes before the meatballs are done, pour the canned tomatoes into a small skillet and mash them with a potato masher or wooden spoon. Season with salt and pepper and cook over medium to medium-high heat to thicken them a bit. ■ Pile the basil, lemon zest, ½ cup parsley leaves, stock, the remaining grated or minced garlic clove, and salt and pepper in the bowl of a food processor. With the processor on, stream in about ¼ cup EVOO until a thick paste forms. ■ When ready to serve, fold the pesto into the thickened tomatoes. Ladle the sauce into shallow bowls and top with meatballs and sprinkle with Parmigiano cheese.

SERVES 4

4 slices of stale white or farmhouse-style bread, torn into pieces

Milk, to moisten the bread

2½ pounds ground beef, pork, and veal mix

3 garlic cloves, grated or minced

A generous handful of fresh flat-leaf parsley leaves, chopped, plus ½ cup leaves

¾ cup grated Parmigiano-Reggiano cheese, 2 handfuls

1 egg

Salt and pepper

16 bocconcini (bite-size mini fresh mozzarella balls) or 1-pound ball cut into 16 cubes

2 tablespoons EVOO (extra-virgin olive oil), plus about ¼ cup

1 (28-ounce) can San Marzano plum tomatoes

1 cup fresh basil leaves, packed

1 teaspoon grated lemon zest

¼ cup vegetable or chicken stock

A shout-out to my friend Adam Perry Lang for teaching me this fabulous method of dressing the steak.

steakhouse rib eyes &
tomato stacks

Bring the steaks to room temperature. ■ Preheat the oven to 375°F. ■ Arrange the bacon on a slotted pan and bake until crisp, 15 to 18 minutes. Cool and chop into large pieces. Set aside. ■ Place a large cast-iron skillet or griddle pan over high heat. ■ Rub the steaks with the cut garlic, coat with a liberal drizzle of EVOO, and season with salt and pepper. ■ When the pan smokes, add the meat and caramelize, cooking for about 4 minutes before flipping. Turn the meat and cook for 4 to 5 minutes more for medium-rare, 8 minutes more for medium-well. Drizzle EVOO on the carving board, transfer the steaks to the board, then let them rest, tented with foil, for the juices to redistribute. ■ While the meat rests, whisk together the crème fraîche, grated or minced garlic, buttermilk, dill, chives, the juice of 1 lemon, horseradish, and salt and pepper to make a thick dressing. Place the onion slices between the tomato halves. Pour dressing over the top and garnish with lots of bacon. ■ Thinly slice the meat against the grain. Dress the sliced meat with parsley, the juice of the second lemon, a few more tablespoons of EVOO, and additional salt and pepper. Serve immediately with the tomato stacks alongside.

SERVES 4

2 big rib-eye steaks, each about 1½ inches thick

8 slices bacon

4 large garlic cloves, 2 halved to rub steaks and 2 grated or minced for the dressing

EVOO (extra-virgin olive oil), for liberal drizzling

Salt and pepper

1 cup crème fraîche or sour cream

½ cup buttermilk

2 tablespoons finely chopped fresh dill

2 tablespoons finely chopped fresh chives

2 lemons

2 tablespoons prepared horseradish

4 (½-inch-thick) slices red onion

4 beefsteak tomatoes, halved horizontally and cored

½ cup curly parsley, stems removed, finely chopped

individual beef wellingtons

SERVES 4

4 (1½-inch-thick) filet mignon steaks

1 tablespoon EVOO (extra-virgin olive oil), **plus some for drizzling**

2 tablespoons butter

½ pound button mushrooms, **wiped clean and finely chopped**

1 large shallot, **finely chopped**

3 to 4 sprigs of fresh thyme, **leaves removed and finely chopped**

Salt **and** pepper

¼ cup dry sherry, **a couple splashes**

8 ounces mousse pâté

1 sheet frozen puff pastry dough, **11 x 17 inches, or 2 smaller sheets—depends on the brand, defrosted**

All-purpose flour

1 egg, **lightly beaten with a splash of water**

4 plum tomatoes, **halved lengthwise**

1 bundle of broccolini, **trimmed and sliced into spears or 1 bunch of broccoli**

Bring the steaks to room temperature. ■ Preheat the oven to 425°F. ■ Heat the oil and butter in a small skillet over medium heat. When the butter melts into the oil, add the mushrooms and cook to darken for 3 to 4 minutes, then add the shallots, thyme, and salt and pepper and cook for a few minutes more. Add the sherry and stir, then remove the mushrooms from the heat and let cool. ■ Drizzle the steaks with EVOO to coat and season with salt and pepper. Heat a skillet over high heat. Add the steaks to the very hot pan and caramelize it for 2 minutes on each side. ■ Cut the pâté into 4 pieces, 2 ounces each. Roll out the puff pastry sheet a bit on a lightly floured surface. If using one large sheet of dough, quarter it, or halve two smaller sheets of dough. Cover a baking sheet with parchment paper and lay out the 4 rectangles of dough. On each rectangle of dough, place one quarter of the cooked mushrooms. Top the mushrooms with a portion of pâté and 1 steak. Wrap the dough up and over the meat, trim the excess dough, and seal with egg wash, using a pastry brush. ■ Leftover dough bits may be used to decorate the tops of your Wellingtons. Turn the wrapped Wellingtons over on the lined baking sheet. Cut small vents into the tops with a knife, and brush evenly with egg wash. Bake for 10 to 15 minutes, or until fluffed and golden. Let stand for 5 minutes, then serve. ■ While the Wellingtons are baking, preheat the broiler to high. Place the plum tomatoes on a rimmed baking sheet. Drizzle with olive oil and salt and pepper. Broil for 5 minutes. ■ Cook the broccolini in 1 inch of simmering salted water, covered, for about 5 minutes or until just tender. ■ Serve the Wellingtons with the tomatoes and broccolini alongside.

My recipe for Individual Beef Wellingtons was first printed about ten years ago. It's my best fake-out dish, so I had to include it in *Look + Cook*.

You'll look like a rock star serving this dish. Only you will know how easy it is to make the salmon. Serve with your choice of vegetable and boiled baby potatoes.

fancy pants salmon

Preheat the oven to 400°F. ■ Place a large skillet over medium-high heat with 1 tablespoon of the EVOO. Season the fish with salt and pepper and sear for a minute on each side. Remove the fish and reserve. Add the remaining tablespoon of EVOO to the skillet. Add the mushrooms and brown for 5 to 6 minutes, then add the leeks and cook until they are softened, 2 to 3 minutes more. Season the mushrooms with salt and pepper, then add the mustard, cream, and tarragon to the skillet. Bring up to a bubble, reduce the heat to medium, and simmer until thickened, 3 minutes. Remove from the heat and let cool. ■ Roll out the puff pastry with a little flour on a large work area. Quarter a large sheet or halve two smaller sheets. Line a baking sheet with parchment paper and arrange the rectangles of dough on it. Divide the mushroom cream sauce among the rectangles of dough, making a small pile in the middle of each. Place a piece of seared fish on top of the sauce and fold the edges of the dough up around the fillet. Trim the excess dough. Use the egg wash to secure the seam, then place the fish seam side down on the lined baking sheet. Cut a few slits in the top of each pastry parcel. Brush them with the egg wash and transfer to the oven. Bake until the pastry is puffed and golden, about 15 to 20 minutes. ■ Serve immediately.

SERVES 4

2 tablespoons EVOO **(extra-virgin olive oil)**

4 skinless salmon fillets

Salt **and** pepper

½ pound button mushrooms, **thinly sliced**

1 or 2 small leeks, **halved lengthwise, thinly sliced into half-moons on an angle, cleaned, and dried**

1 tablespoon Dijon mustard

¾ cup heavy cream

2 tablespoons chopped fresh tarragon leaves

1 sheet frozen puff pastry dough, **11 x 17, or 2 smaller sheets— depends on the brand, defrosted**

All-purpose flour

1 egg, **lightly beaten with a splash of water**

sliced chicken with apples, pears & camembert mashed potatoes

Halve the small and quarter the larger baby potatoes into bite-size pieces and cover with water in a large pot. Bring the water to a boil and season with salt. Cook for 12 to 15 minutes until the potatoes are fork-tender. ■ Heat the EVOO in a large nonstick skillet over medium-high heat. Season the chicken with salt and pepper on both sides and cook the chicken until golden and firm, about 12 minutes, turning once. Place the chicken on a plate and cover with foil to keep warm. ■ In the same skillet melt the butter over medium heat; add the apples and pears and season with salt and the nutmeg. Stir in the lemon juice and cook for 5 minutes, or until tender-crisp, then stir in the honey and cook for a minute more. ■ Drain the potatoes and return them to the hot pot. Mash them with the cheese and milk or half-and-half and season with salt and pepper to taste. Divide the potatoes among 4 plates. Slice the chicken breasts on an angle. Arrange the sliced chicken alongside the potatoes and top with the apples and pears. Combine the chives with the thyme and lemon zest and scatter over each plate.

SERVES 4

2 pounds baby Yukon Gold potatoes

Salt

1 tablespoon EVOO (extra-virgin olive oil)

4 pieces boneless skinless chicken breast

Black pepper

2 tablespoons butter, **cut into small pieces**

1 Gala, Honey Crisp, or Golden Delicious apple, **peeled, cored, and cut into ½-inch dice**

1 Bosc pear, **peeled, cored, and diced**

Freshly grated nutmeg, **¼ teaspoon**

Zest and juice of 1 lemon

2 tablespoons honey

⅓ pound ripe Camembert **cheese, diced into bite-size pieces**

¼ to ⅓ cup milk, **half-and-half, or cream**

10 to 12 blades of chives, **chopped**

2 tablespoons fresh thyme leaves, **finely chopped**

french onion dip pizza

SERVES 4

2 tablespoons **EVOO** (extra-virgin olive oil), **plus extra for brushing**

2 large onions, **thinly sliced**

2 garlic cloves, **finely chopped or grated**

1 ball of fresh pizza dough, **about 16 ounces (1 pound)**

Salt **and** pepper

1 cup crème fraîche **or sour cream**

¾ cup shredded sharp white cheddar **cheese**

¾ cup shredded Gruyère **cheese**

½ cup grated Parmigiano-Reggiano **cheese**

1 tablespoon fresh thyme leaves, **chopped**

Preheat the oven to 450°F. ■ Place a large skillet over medium heat with the EVOO. Add the onions to the pan and gently cook, stirring occasionally, until the onions are soft and deep golden brown, about 25 minutes. Stir in the garlic for the last 8 to 10 minutes of cooking time. ■ While the onions are cooking, stretch out the pizza dough to the size of the pan. Transfer the dough onto the pan, brush with a little EVOO, bake until set and very light golden brown, about 15 minutes. ■ When the onions are ready, season with salt and pepper and stir in the crème fraîche or sour cream. Spread this mixture over the prebaked pizza crust. Sprinkle the three cheeses and thyme over the pizza and return it to the oven. Bake until the top is golden brown and the cheese is bubbly, about 10 minutes.

marsala burgers

SERVES 4

1 **pound** ground sirloin

1 **pound** ground veal

2 **garlic cloves, grated or finely chopped**

Freshly grated nutmeg, about ¼ teaspoon

Salt **and** pepper

¼ **cup fresh** flat-leaf parsley **leaves, a handful, finely chopped**

3 **tablespoons** EVOO **(extra-virgin olive oil)**

4 **portabella mushroom caps, thinly sliced**

2 **tablespoons fresh** thyme leaves, **chopped**

½ **cup** Marsala

2 **tablespoons** butter

4 **crusty kaiser or ciabatta** rolls, split

A chunk of Parmigiano-Reggiano **cheese, for shaving**

In a mixing bowl, combine the ground meats with the garlic, nutmeg, salt and pepper, and chopped parsley. Score the meat into 4 equal portions, then form patties thicker at the edges and thinner at the center for even cooking. ■ Preheat a large nonstick skillet with 1 tablespoon of the EVOO over medium-high heat. Add the patties to the hot skillet and cook for about 8 minutes total for medium-rare, 10 minutes for medium, or 12 minutes for well-done, turning once. ■ Meanwhile, heat a medium skillet over medium-high heat with the remaining 2 tablespoons of EVOO. Add the mushrooms to the hot oil and sauté until golden brown. Season with salt, pepper, and the thyme. (Hold off seasoning until the mushrooms are brown because the salt will draw out liquids that would otherwise slow down the browning process.) Douse the pan with the Marsala and reduce for 30 seconds, then add the butter, melt, and turn off the heat. ■ If the rolls are not super-crusty, warm them in the oven on low heat. ■ To assemble, place a patty on the roll bottom and top with mounds of Marsala mushrooms. Using a vegetable peeler, shave a few curls of Parmigiano on top of the mushrooms and set the roll top in place.

Piquillo peppers are small, mild **Spanish peppers** and are available in many markets next to **roasted red bell peppers**. If they are not available, roasted red bell peppers may be substituted.

piquillo pepper chicken
with spanish rice

In a small pan over medium heat, lightly toast the almonds and reserve. ■ In a small saucepan, bring the broth, raisins, 1 tablespoon of the EVOO, the turmeric, and the saffron to a boil. Stir in the rice, cover the pot, and simmer over low heat for 18 minutes, or until the rice is cooked through and the liquid is absorbed. ■ While the rice cooks, in a large skillet, heat the remaining 2 tablespoons of EVOO, over medium-high heat. Season the chicken liberally with salt and pepper, add to the skillet, and cook for 6 minutes on each side. Transfer to a plate and keep warm. Add the piquillo peppers to the pan and heat through, about 2 minutes. Add the sherry and boil for 1 to 2 minutes until slightly reduced. Add the butter and half the parsley and turn off the heat, stirring to melt the butter. Spoon the sauce over the chicken. ■ Add the remaining parsley and the almonds to the rice and fluff with a fork. Serve the rice alongside the chicken.

SERVES 4

½ **cup** sliced almonds

3 **cups** chicken stock

1 **small handful of** golden raisins

3 **tablespoons** EVOO **(extra-virgin olive oil)**

1 **teaspoon ground** turmeric

2 **pinches of** saffron threads **or approximately 1 small envelope saffron powder**

1½ **cups** white rice

4 **boneless skinless** chicken breast **halves, 6 ounces each**

Salt **and** pepper

1 **small jar** piquillo peppers **in water, 4 to 5 peppers, or 2 jarred roasted red peppers, drained and sliced**

½ **cup** dry sherry

2 **tablespoons** butter, **chilled and cut into pieces**

½ **cup fresh** flat-leaf parsley **leaves, a couple handfuls, finely chopped**

cod & shrimp stoup with
salt & vinegar mashed potatoes

Place the potatoes in a pot, cover with water, and bring to a boil. Salt the water and cook the potatoes until tender, about 15 minutes. ■ Heat the EVOO in a Dutch oven or large deep skillet over medium to medium-high heat. When the oil is hot, add the onions, celery, garlic, bay leaf, thyme, and lemon zest. Season with salt and pepper and cook until the onions and celery are tender, 7 to 8 minutes. Deglaze the pan with the wine and stir for 1 minute. Add ¼ cup of the stock and the tomatoes and bring to a bubble. Add the cod, cover, cook for 3 to 4 minutes, then stir in the shrimp, season with salt and pepper, cover again, and cook for 3 to 4 minutes more. Remove the lid, stir in the lemon juice, and remove the bay leaf. ■ Drain the potatoes and return them to the hot pot. Mash the potatoes with the vinegar, the remaining ¼ cup of stock, and the butter. Season with salt to taste. ■ To serve, spoon or scoop the potatoes into mounds in shallow bowls, then ladle the stoup around the potatoes.

SERVES 4

4 large Idaho potatoes, **peeled and thickly sliced**

Salt

3 tablespoons EVOO **(extra-virgin olive oil)**

2 onions, **thinly sliced**

3 to 4 celery stalks **from the heart with leafy tops, chopped**

3 to 4 garlic cloves, **finely chopped**

1 large fresh bay leaf

2 tablespoons fresh thyme leaves, **from several sprigs, chopped**

Zest and juice of 1 lemon

Black pepper

½ cup dry white wine

1 cup chicken stock

1 (15-ounce) can diced tomatoes **or** stewed tomatoes

1½ pounds cod, **cut into chunks (ask for thick pieces)**

1 pound large shrimp, **peeled and deveined**

¼ cup white balsamic vinegar **or** white wine vinegar

2 tablespoons butter

greek salad stack
with sliced steak

1½ **pounds** beef sirloin **or boneless lamb leg steaks, 1 inch thick**

EVOO (extra-virgin olive oil), for brushing pita, plus 3 tablespoons

4 **pita breads, torn**

Salt

1 **teaspoon fresh** oregano **leaves**

1 **teaspoon** crushed red pepper flakes

Black pepper

1 **cup plain** Greek yogurt

1 **small** garlic clove**, grated or finely chopped**

2 lemons

½ **teaspoon ground** cumin**, eyeball it in your palm**

½ **cup crumbled** feta cheese

2 romaine lettuce hearts**, shredded**

6 plum tomatoes**, coarsely chopped**

½ seedless cucumber**, chopped into 1-inch cubes**

1 **small** red onion**, chopped into 1-inch cubes**

1 green bell pepper**, seeded and chopped into 1-inch cubes**

1 **cup fresh** flat-leaf parsley **leaves, loosely packed**

Peperoncini**, for garnish**

Kalamata olives**, for garnish**

Remove the meat from the refrigerator to take the chill off. ■ Heat a grill pan or cast-iron skillet to high. ■ Preheat the oven to 400°F. Pour some EVOO into a small dish. Arrange the pita on a baking sheet. Brush the pita lightly with oil, season with salt, oregano, and red pepper flakes, and bake until crisp, 10 to 12 minutes. ■ Rub the meat with 1 tablespoon of EVOO and season with salt and black pepper. Grill the meat for 3 to 4 minutes on each side for medium doneness and let it rest for 10 minutes, keeping warm, before slicing. ■ While the meat cooks, combine the yogurt, garlic, juice of 1 lemon, cumin, and feta in a food processor. Process the yogurt dressing until smooth. Add a tablespoon or two of water if necessary; the dressing should be thick but good for pouring. ■ Add the lettuce to a serving platter or a glass casserole or bowl and dress with the juice of the remaining lemon, the remaining 2 tablespoons of EVOO, and salt and black pepper. Top the lettuce with the crispy pita, then top with the tomatoes, cucumber, onions, bell pepper, and parsley. Drizzle the dressing evenly over the vegetables. Arrange the warm sliced meat atop the salad, garnish with peperoncini and olives, and serve immediately.

knife & fork burgers with stewed vegetable gravy

Heat about 1½ tablespoons of the EVOO in a sauce pot over medium heat. Add the potatoes, carrots, celery, and onions to the pot as you chop them. ■ Season with the bay leaf, thyme, and salt and pepper and cover the pot to sweat the vegetables for 10 minutes. Uncover the pot and stir in the tomato paste for 1 minute. Make a well in the center of the pot and add the butter. When the butter is melted, stir in the flour for 1 minute more, then add the stock. Bring the stew-gravy to a simmer and reduce the heat to low. Cook for 5 minutes more, or until the vegetables are tender. Discard the bay leaf. ■ While the vegetables cook, mix the meat with parsley, Worcestershire, and salt and pepper. Form 4 large patties that are thinner at the center and thicker at the edges for even cooking. Heat the remaining ½ tablespoon of EVOO in a large cast-iron or nonstick skillet over medium-high heat. Cook the patties for 8 minutes, turning once, for pink centers, a minute less for rare, or 2 minutes more for well-done. ■ While the meat cooks, toast and butter the muffins. ■ Place the burgers on muffin halves on plates and spoon the stew over top. Garnish with cheese crumbles and chives, if you like.

SERVES 4

2 tablespoons EVOO (extra-virgin olive oil)

6 fingerling potatoes, thinly sliced

2 small or 1 medium carrot, chopped

2 small celery stalks, from the heart, chopped

1 small yellow onion, chopped

1 bay leaf, fresh or dried

A few sprigs of fresh thyme, leaves removed and chopped

Salt and pepper

1 tablespoon tomato paste

2 tablespoons butter, plus some for buttering the English muffins

2 tablespoons all-purpose flour

2 cups beef stock

2 pounds ground sirloin—ask your butcher for a coarse grind

2 handfuls of fresh flat-leaf parsley leaves, about ½ cup, finely chopped

¼ cup Worcestershire sauce (eyeball it)

2 sandwich-size sourdough English muffins, split

Extra-sharp aged white cheddar crumbles, for garnish (optional)

Chopped fresh chives, for garnish (optional)

bacon-wrapped halibut,
shredded brussels sprouts & sour cream & chive mashed potatoes

Halve the potatoes and place in a pot. Cover the potatoes with water, bring to a boil, then salt the water and cook the potatoes until tender, 10 to 12 minutes. ■ Preheat the oven to 375°F. ■ Halve the Brussels sprouts, place them cut side down on a cutting board, thinly slice lengthwise, and reserve. ■ While the potatoes cook, season the fish with Old Bay and wrap the fish with bacon. Heat ½ tablespoon of the vegetable oil over medium-high heat in an ovenproof skillet. When the oil is hot, add the fish and cook for 2 minutes on each side to crisp up the bacon, then transfer to the oven for 7 to 8 minutes to cook through. ■ While the fish cooks, heat the remaining 2 tablespoons of oil in a large skillet over high heat. Add the sliced Brussels sprouts and toss to coat in the oil. Season with salt and pepper and cook for 2 to 3 minutes, then add the shallots, bell pepper, garlic, and thyme. Toss for a minute or two more, then add about ½ cup of the stock and cook it out for 2 to 3 minutes more. Turn off the heat and melt in the butter, then garnish with the tarragon. ■ Drain the potatoes and return them to the hot pot. Mash with the sour cream, the chives, the remaining ¼ cup of stock, and salt and pepper to taste. ■ Serve the fish on the Brussels sprouts with mashers and a wedge of lemon alongside.

SERVES 4

2 pounds baby Yukon Gold potatoes

Salt

1 pound Brussels sprouts

4 (6- to 8-ounce) skinless halibut fillets

2 teaspoons Old Bay seafood seasoning

4 slices smoky bacon

2½ tablespoons vegetable oil

Black pepper

1 large shallot**, thinly sliced**

½ red bell pepper**, seeded and chopped**

2 garlic cloves**, finely chopped**

A few sprigs of fresh thyme**, leaves removed and chopped**

¾ cup chicken stock

1 tablespoon butter**, cut into pieces**

A few stems of fresh tarragon**, leaves removed and chopped**

½ cup sour cream

¼ to ⅓ cup chopped fresh chives

4 lemon **wedges**

salmon fillets with
dill couscous & spicy kale

SERVES 4

3 tablespoons EVOO (extra-virgin olive oil)

1 red onion, **chopped**

½ teaspoon crushed red pepper flakes

1 bunch of kale, **stemmed and chopped, ½ to ⅔ pound**

Salt **and** pepper

Freshly grated nutmeg

2¼ cups chicken stock

3 to 4 radishes, **thinly sliced**

1 lemon

4 skinless salmon fillets

1 tablespoon Old Bay seafood seasoning

1 tablespoon butter

1¼ cups couscous

¼ cup chopped fresh dill

¼ seedless cucumber, **cut into ¼-inch dice**

Heat 2 **tablespoons** of the EVOO in a skillet with a lid over medium to medium-high heat. Add the onions and cook for 3 to 4 minutes. Add the red pepper flakes, wilt in the kale, and season with salt, pepper, and nutmeg. Pour in 1 cup of the stock, cover, and simmer for 10 to 12 minutes. Then uncover, add the radishes, and sprinkle with the juice of ½ lemon. ■ While the kale cooks, heat the remaining tablespoon of EVOO in a skillet over medium-high heat. Season the salmon with Old Bay. Cook for 2 to 3 minutes on each side for pink centers and 2 minutes longer on each side for opaque fish. Douse the fish with the juice of the remaining ½ lemon. ■ While the salmon cooks, bring the remaining 1¼ cups of stock and the butter to a boil in a rice or sauce pot with a lid. Once it is boiling, stir in the couscous and dill. Turn off the heat, cover, and let stand for 5 minutes. Fluff with a fork. ■ Serve the salmon on a bed of spicy kale and couscous. Garnish the dill couscous with the chopped cucumber.

This is a hearty meal as is, but if you're entertaining, add the **Green Beans with Crispy Bacon** on page 275.

beer-braised shrimp with louisiana salsa & rice

In a medium bowl, combine the garlic, celery, bell peppers, onions, and thyme. ■ Heat a medium pot with 1 tablespoon of the butter over medium heat. Add about one third of the vegetables to the pot, cook for 2 to 3 minutes to soften, then add the rice and toss around for another 1 to 2 minutes. Stir in the chicken stock, cover the pot, and bring to a boil. Simmer the rice for 15 to 18 minutes, until tender, then fluff with a fork. ■ Combine the remaining vegetables with the jalapeño pepper and tomatoes, dress with the juice of 1 lime, and season with a little salt. ■ Heat the EVOO in a large skillet over medium-high to high heat. Add the shrimp and season with the Old Bay, Worcestershire sauce, and hot sauce. Toss the shrimp around for 2 minutes, add the beer, reduce the heat to a simmer, and braise for 5 to 6 minutes. Cut the remaining 3 tablespoons of butter into small bits, then add the scallions and melt the butter into the sauce. Squeeze the juice of the second lime over the pan. ■ Serve the shrimp on plates topped with a generous scoop of rice and garnished with generous spoonfuls of salsa. If you prefer lots of rice, reverse the order and fill the plate with rice, then top with the shrimp and salsa.

SERVES 6

4 garlic cloves, **grated or finely chopped**

6 to 8 small celery stalks **from the heart, chopped**

1 large or 2 medium green bell peppers, **seeded and chopped**

1 medium to large red onion, **chopped**

2 tablespoons finely chopped fresh thyme leaves

4 tablespoons (½ stick) butter

1½ cups enriched white rice

2½ cups chicken stock

1 red jalapeño pepper, **very thinly sliced**

½ pint small tomatoes (cherry, **grape, or small heirlooms), halved**

2 limes

Salt

2 tablespoons EVOO (extra-virgin olive oil)

3 pounds large shrimp, deveined, **tail on**

1 tablespoon Old Bay seafood seasoning

1 tablespoon Worcestershire sauce

¼ cup hot sauce

1 bottle of beer

1 bunch of scallions, **thinly sliced on an angle**

veal & olive ragù
with pappardelle

SERVES 6

Salt

1 pound pappardelle **or other wide, flat pasta**

2 tablespoons EVOO **(extra-virgin olive oil)**

1 tablespoon butter

1½ pounds ground veal

Black pepper

1 onion, finely chopped

2 garlic cloves, **finely chopped**

2 tablespoons tomato paste

2 sprigs of fresh rosemary, **leaves removed and finely chopped**

1 cup pitted large green olives, **coarsely chopped**

½ cup dry white wine

1 cup beef broth

⅓ cup finely chopped fresh flat-leaf parsley **leaves (a generous handful)**

2 teaspoons finely grated lemon zest

½ cup grated Pecorino Romano **cheese, plus more for passing at the table**

Bring a large pot of water to a boil, salt it, then add the pasta, cook to al dente, and drain. ■ While the pasta is cooking, in a large, deep skillet, heat the EVOO over medium-high heat. Add the butter to melt, then add the veal and season with salt and a little pepper. Cook, breaking up the meat with a wooden spoon, until it's no longer pink, about 5 minutes. Add the onions and garlic and cook, stirring occasionally, until softened, about 5 minutes. Stir in the tomato paste and rosemary and cook for 2 minutes, then stir in the olives and heat through for 1 minute. Stir in the wine, scraping up the browned bits from the bottom of the pan for 1 minute. Stir in the beef broth and simmer for 2 minutes. Stir in the parsley and lemon zest. ■ Add the drained pasta to the sauce and stir in the pasta and ½ cup of cheese. Serve hot with extra cheese.

pork chops with balsamic strawberry salad & orzo

Bring a pot of water to a boil for the orzo. Salt the water and cook the pasta to al dente. ■ Place the balsamic vinegar in a small pot and bring to a boil. Reduce the vinegar by half or until it is a syrupy consistency. This will take 5 to 6 minutes. ■ Combine the strawberries, basil, and spinach in a bowl, then pour the balsamic drizzle over the top and stir gently. ■ Heat a drizzle of EVOO in a medium nonstick skillet over medium-high heat and add the prosciutto strips. Cook for 4 to 5 minutes, remove with a slotted spoon to a paper-towel-lined plate, and reserve. Add another drizzle of oil to the pan. Season the chops with salt and pepper and cook for 4 minutes on each side. Place a loose foil tent over the pan to avoid splatter and reflect some of the heat. ■ In a second larger skillet, toast the nuts over medium heat, shaking the pan often. When lightly golden, after 3 to 4 minutes, remove the nuts to a plate. Return the skillet to the stove, add the butter, then drain the pasta. When the butter begins to brown, add the pasta, toss, then season with salt, cinnamon, and nutmeg to taste. Stir in the nuts. ■ Serve the chops with orzo alongside and salad atop the chops. Garnish with the crisp prosciutto.

SERVES 4

Salt

½ pound orzo pasta

½ cup balsamic vinegar

1 pint strawberries, **hulled and quartered lengthwise**

½ cup fresh basil leaves, **torn or thinly sliced**

1 cup baby spinach leaves, **thinly sliced**

EVOO (extra-virgin olive oil), for drizzling

4 slices prosciutto di Parma, **sliced into ½-inch strips**

4 (1-inch-thick) bone-in pork chops

Black pepper

¼ cup pine nuts, **a generous handful**

3 tablespoons butter

Pinch of ground cinnamon

Freshly grated nutmeg

turkey meat loaf burgers
with cranberry sauce & white cheddar

Heat a large skillet over medium heat. Melt the butter and add the chopped onions, celery, and apple, then season with salt and pepper and cook for 3 to 4 minutes under a loose foil tent. Stir in the bread crumbs and transfer to a bowl to cool a bit. Add the meat, poultry seasoning, salt, pepper, parsley, mustard, and the egg and mix. Form 4 burgers. Wipe out the skillet and heat a liberal drizzle of EVOO in it over medium-high heat. Cook the patties for 11 to 12 minutes until cooked through. Melt the cheddar over the tops of the burgers during the last minute or two of cooking. ■ While the burgers cook, toast the split English muffins under the broiler or in the toaster. ■ Mix together in a small bowl the cranberry sauce, sour cream, and chives. ■ Serve the burgers on English muffins with red onion, lettuce, and the cranberry sauce.

SERVES 4

4 tablespoons (½ stick) butter

1 small or ½ medium onion, finely chopped

1 small celery stalk, finely chopped

1 small McIntosh apple, peeled, cored, and finely chopped

Salt and pepper

⅓ cup bread crumbs, rounded handful

1 pound ground turkey with some or all dark meat, not breast

2 teaspoons poultry seasoning, ⅔ palmful

¼ cup chopped fresh flat-leaf parsley leaves

2 tablespoons Dijon mustard

1 medium egg

EVOO (extra-virgin olive oil), for drizzling

4 slices sharp white cheddar, for topping the burgers

4 sandwich-size sourdough English muffins

⅓ cup whole-berry cranberry sauce

3 tablespoons sour cream

2 tablespoons chopped fresh chives

4 thin slices raw red onion

4 red leaf or red romaine lettuce leaves

individual florentine
frying-pan pizza

SERVES 1

3 tablespoons EVOO (extra-virgin olive oil)

½ pound cremini mushrooms, sliced

Salt and pepper

2 tablespoons butter

2 garlic cloves, grated or minced

2 tablespoons all-purpose flour

½ cup milk

Freshly grated nutmeg

1 (10-ounce) box frozen chopped spinach, thawed and squeezed dry in a clean kitchen towel

1 pound store-bought pizza dough, quartered

1 cup shredded Italian Fontina or Provolone cheese

¼ cup grated Parmigiano-Reggiano cheese, a handful

Preheat the oven to 425°F. ■ Heat a medium nonstick skillet over medium-high heat with 2 tablespoons of the EVOO. Add the mushrooms and sauté until golden brown. Season them with salt and pepper, then remove to a plate. Lower the heat to medium-low, then add the butter to the pan and melt. Add the garlic and stir for 1 minute, then sprinkle the flour into the pan and whisk for a minute. Whisk in the milk and season with salt, pepper, and nutmeg. ■ Add the mushrooms back to the skillet and stir them into the sauce. Separate the drained defrosted spinach with your fingers to loosen it up as you add it to the pan. Stir the spinach into the mushrooms and sauce. Remove from the heat. ■ Roll out ¼ pound of pizza dough to form a round large enough to cover the bottom and sides of a 6-inch skillet. Wrap and freeze the unused pizza dough in ¼-pound individual portions. Heads up: If your skillet handle isn't oven-safe, wrap the handle a couple of times with aluminum foil. Drizzle the remaining tablespoon of EVOO into the skillet and coat the sides with a pastry brush. Lay the dough into the skillet, pressing gently as you work the dough up the sides so it reaches the edge of the skillet. Fill the dough with the mushroom and spinach mixture and top with Fontina or Provolone and the Parmigiano cheeses. Pop in the oven and bake for 35 to 45 minutes, until the edges and bottom of the crust are golden brown.

This is a deep-dish delight. I love to make this when I'm home alone and the weather outside is lousy. I curl up, watch a movie with my puppy, and pass out in a blissful pizza-induced food coma.

This meal is complete with some **steamed veggies** alongside.

chicken breasts
with chestnut stovetop stuffing & balsamic cream gravy

Place a large skillet over medium-high heat with 2 tablespoons of the EVOO. Season the chicken breasts with salt and pepper and sear in the hot skillet until golden brown and cooked through, 4 to 5 minutes per side. ■ While the chicken is cooking, place a small skillet over medium-high heat with the remaining 2 tablespoons of EVOO. Cook the leeks in the pan until tender, 4 to 5 minutes. Season with salt and pepper, add the chestnuts and about ½ cup of the stock to the pan, and bring up to a bubble. ■ While the leeks are cooking, toast the bread and spread with about 2 tablespoons of the butter. Chop the toast into 1-inch cubes and transfer to a large bowl. Add the leeks, chestnuts, parsley, and thyme to the bread cubes and toss to combine, then cover with foil. ■ Place a small pot over medium-high heat with the remaining 2 tablespoons of butter. Sprinkle the flour over the melted butter and cook for about a minute. Whisk in the remaining cup of chicken stock, the cream, and the balsamic vinegar, and bring up to a bubble. Simmer for 2 to 3 minutes until thickened, and season with salt and pepper. ■ Serve the chicken breasts with the stuffing and balsamic cream gravy.

SERVES 4

4 tablespoons EVOO (extra-virgin olive oil)

4 boneless skinless chicken breast halves, 6 ounches each

Salt and pepper

2 leeks, halved lengthwise, thinly sliced into half-moons, cleaned, and dried

1 cup chopped chestnuts, jarred or fresh roasted

1½ cups chicken stock, divided

4 (1-inch-thick) slices brioche or challah bread

4 tablespoons (1 stick) butter, divided

¼ cup fresh flat-leaf parsley leaves, chopped

1 tablespoon fresh thyme leaves, from a few sprigs

2 tablespoons all-purpose flour

⅓ to ½ cup heavy cream

2 tablespoons aged balsamic vinegar

double-bacon beer-braised cheeseburgers

SERVES 4

10 slices smoky bacon**, 2 of them chopped**

1 tablespoon EVOO **(extra-virgin olive oil)**

1 small onion**, finely chopped (about ¼ cup)**

¾ pound ground chuck

¾ pound ground sirloin

2 tablespoons Worcestershire sauce

Salt **and** pepper

A few hearty glugs of stout beer**, such as Guinness, ½ bottle**

½ pound sharp aged white cheddar **cheese, sliced**

½ cup sour cream

1 tablespoon prepared horseradish

3 tablespoons grainy mustard

4 kaiser rolls **or crusty rolls, split open**

8 red leaf lettuce **or red leaf romaine leaves**

1 red onion**, sliced**

Preheat the oven to 350°F. ■ Arrange the 8 whole slices of bacon on a slotted broiler pan and bake until crisp, 15 to 20 minutes. ■ Place a large skillet over medium heat with the EVOO. While the pan is still cold, add the chopped bacon. Cook the bacon as the pan heats up until crispy and golden brown, 3 to 4 minutes. When the bacon is crispy, add the onions and continue cooking until tender, 5 to 6 minutes more. Using a slotted spoon to drain off the excess oil, transfer the mixture to a large mixing bowl and cool. Reserve the pan drippings. ■ Reheat the skillet to medium-high heat. Combine the ground meat with the cooled bacon and onions, the Worcestershire, and salt and pepper and form 4 large patties, thinner at the center and thicker at the edges for even cooking. Add the patties to the hot drippings and cook 8 minutes for medium rare, 10 for pink centers, and 12 minutes for medium-well, turning once. About a minute after the burgers have been flipped, add the beer to the skillet. In the last minute, top the burgers with cheese and tent with foil to help melt the cheese. ■ While the burgers cook, combine the sour cream, horseradish, and mustard in a small bowl. ■ Set the cheeseburgers on the roll bottoms, top with a crisscross of bacon, garnish with lettuce leaves, red onion, and horseradish sauce, then set the roll tops in place.

Nicknamed **"The Adirondacker,"** this burger is dedicated to Jake and the gang at Oscar's Smokehouse in Warrensburg, New York.

super-sized 7-layer casserole

SERVES 10 TO 12

1 package large flour tortillas

Cooking spray

Salt

1 box elbow macaroni **with ridges or cavatappi pasta (hollow corkscrews with ridges)**

1 tablespoon EVOO **(extra-virgin olive oil)**

2 pounds ground beef

1 medium onion, **finely chopped**

6 garlic cloves, **finely chopped**

4 jalapeño peppers, **finely chopped**

3 tablespoons tomato paste

2 tablespoons chili powder

1 tablespoon ground coriander

1 tablespoon ground cumin

1 bottle of beer **or 1½ cups chicken stock**

3 tablespoons butter

3 tablespoons all-purpose flour

Preheat the oven to 400°F. ■ Slice the tortillas into 1-inch strips. Coat with cooking spray and scatter on a rimmed baking sheet. Bake until crisp and light golden in color, about 10 minutes, then season with salt and reserve. ■ Bring a large pot of water to a boil over high heat. Salt the water, then add the pasta and cook to al dente. Drain well. ■ Place a large skillet over medium-high heat with the EVOO. Brown the meat, then add the onions, 4 of the chopped garlic cloves, and 2 of the chopped jalapeños, and cook until the onions are tender. Season the mixture with the tomato paste, chili powder, coriander, and cumin. Let the mixture cook for a minute or two, then add the beer or stock and reduce the heat to a simmer. ■ While the meat is cooking, make the cheese sauce. In a sauce pot over medium heat, melt the butter. Add the flour and whisk for a minute, then add the milk. Cook until thickened enough to coat the back of a

spoon, 3 to 4 minutes. Melt in 2½ cups of the cheese, then fold in the tomatoes with chiles. Pour the sauce over the drained pasta, toss, and season with salt and pepper to taste. ■ In a medium skillet, heat the refried beans with a splash of water over medium heat. ■ To build the casserole, spread the beef mixture out in the bottom of a 9 x 13-inch casserole dish. Spread the refried beans in an even layer, then spoon on the mac 'n' cheese and sprinkle the reserved ½ cup cheese over the top. Pop the casserole into the oven and bake until golden brown, 15 to 20 minutes. ■ While the casserole is baking, make the salsa by combining the plum tomatoes, remaining jalapeño peppers, red onion, and cilantro in a small bowl. Season the salsa with salt, the zest of 1 lime, and the juice of 2 limes. ■ For the guacamole sour cream, scoop the flesh of the avocados into the bowl of a food processor and add the sour cream, lemon juice, the remaining 2 garlic cloves, and hot sauce to taste. Process until creamy. ■ When the casserole comes out of the oven, top it with the crispy corn strips and shredded iceberg lettuce. Top the lettuce with the salsa, add dollops of guacamole sour cream, and finally, sprinkle with the chopped olives with pimientos and chopped scallions.

2½ cups milk

3 cups shredded sharp yellow cheddar cheese

1 (14.5-ounce) can chopped tomatoes with chiles, drained

Black pepper

2 (14-ounce) cans vegetarian spicy refried beans

5 to 6 plum tomatoes, seeded and diced

1 small red onion, finely chopped

¼ cup fresh cilantro leaves, finely chopped

2 limes

2 ripe Hass avocados

1 cup sour cream

Juice of 1 lemon

Hot sauce

½ head of iceberg lettuce, shredded

½ cup chopped olives with pimientos

1 small bunch of scallions, chopped, whites and greens

MORE
RECIPES!

4

30-minute meals

Many times a year, even after almost a decade of 30-Minute Meals on the Food Network, people will stop me in the grocery store or at a book signing and ask, "Are those *really* thirty-minute meals?" Yes, they are. The food shown on *30-Minute Meals* is mine, not a bunch of swap-outs made ahead for close-ups by an army of kitchen elves. And yes, each meal can be prepared in about thirty minutes. But you don't have to take my word for it any longer. Watch and see for yourself some of these recipes being prepared online in streaming video at RachaelRay.com. Grab the groceries ahead of time and cook along with me as we get dinner on the table in thirty minutes or less! You *always* have time for a great meal.

make your own takeout
cashew chicken or pork
with orange sauce & scallion rice

In a covered sauce pot, heat 1½ cups of the stock and 1 tablespoon of the vegetable oil. Bring to a boil and stir in the rice, bring back to a bubble, cover, and simmer for 18 minutes, or until the rice is tender. Fluff with a fork and add the scallions. ■ Meanwhile, thinly slice the chicken or pork. ■ Trim the broccolini or broccoli and cut into 2-inch pieces or florets. Bring 2 inches of water to a boil in a shallow pot or deep skillet. Salt the water and cook the broccolini or florets for 3 to 4 minutes until tender-crisp, then drain. ■ Heat a large skillet to high heat while the broccolini cooks. Add ½ tablespoon of the oil and when it begins to smoke or ripple, add the chicken and brown for 5 to 6 minutes, turning once, then transfer to a plate. Add the remaining ½ tablespoon of oil to the pan and stir in the ginger and garlic for 1 minute, then stir in 3 tablespoons of the tamari, the marmalade, and the remaining ½ cup of chicken stock. Slide the chicken, broccolini, and cashews into the pan and combine with the sauce. Simmer for another minute or two. ■ Scoop the chicken mixture into dishes, top with a scoop of rice, and serve.

SERVES 4

2 cups **chicken stock**

2 tablespoons canola, vegetable, or other high-temperature cooking **oil**

1 cup **white rice**

1 small bunch of **scallions**, thinly sliced on an angle

6 **chicken cutlets** or chicken thighs or 6 thin pork loin chops

1 large bundle of **broccolini** or 1 head of broccoli

Salt

1½ inches fresh **gingerroot**, peeled and finely chopped or grated

2 to 3 **garlic** cloves, finely chopped

3 tablespoons **tamari** (aged soy sauce)

⅓ cup **orange marmalade**

½ cup roasted unsalted **cashews**

chicken fans with
tarragon-cream sauce
& rice pilaf with asparagus

SERVES 4

4 tablespoons (½ stick) **butter**

¼ cup **orzo pasta** or broken thin spaghetti

1 cup **white rice**

2¾ cups **chicken stock**

1 small bundle of fresh **asparagus**, trimmed and cut into 1-inch pieces on an angle

2 tablespoons **EVOO** (extra-virgin olive oil)

4 pieces boneless skinless **chicken breast**

Salt and **pepper**

2 large **shallots**, chopped

8 medium-large **white mushrooms**, thinly sliced

2 tablespoons all-purpose **flour**

⅓ to ½ cup **cream** (eyeball it)

2 tablespoons **Dijon mustard** or grainy mustard

4 stems of fresh **tarragon**, leaves removed and chopped

Heat a sauce pot with a tight-fitting lid over medium heat with 2 tablespoons of the butter. Add the orzo to the pot and sauté to golden brown. Add the rice and stir to combine. Add 1¾ cups of the stock and bring to a boil, then reduce the heat to a simmer, cover the pot, and cook for 18 minutes, or until the pasta and rice are tender. Add the asparagus to the pot for the last 5 to 6 minutes of cooking time, stirring it in and replacing the lid. When the rice is done, fluff with a fork. ■ While the rice cooks, heat the EVOO in a skillet over medium-high heat. Season the chicken with salt and pepper and cook for 12 minutes, turning once. Place the meat on a platter and cover with foil to keep warm. Add the remaining 2 tablespoons of butter to the pan and reduce the heat to medium. Add the shallots and mushrooms to the skillet and sauté for 6 to 7 minutes, until the mushrooms are very tender, then season with a little salt and pepper. Sprinkle the flour over the pan and stir for 1 minute then whisk in the remaining cup of stock. When the stock comes to a bubble, stir in the cream, mustard, and tarragon and reduce the heat to low. ■ Thinly slice each chicken breast on an angle. Place some pilaf on each plate and fan the chicken out over the edge of the pilaf. Ladle the cream sauce over the chicken fans and serve.

chicken & porcini shepherd's pie with fontina-sage potatoes

Place the potatoes in a pot, cover with water, and bring to a boil. Salt the water and cook until the potatoes are fork-tender, 12 to 15 minutes. When tender, drain the potatoes and return to the hot pot. Mash the potatoes with the milk or cream, sage, salt and pepper, and the cheese. Add nutmeg to taste and stir in the egg. ■ While the potatoes come to a boil, place the porcinis in a small pot and cover with the stock. Place over medium heat, bring to a boil, then reduce the heat to low and simmer to reconstitute the mushrooms. ■ While the mushrooms are softening, heat the EVOO in a skillet over medium-high heat, place an oven rack in the center of the oven, and preheat the broiler. Add the pancetta to the hot oil and crisp for 2 to 3 minutes, then add the chicken and cook for 5 to 6 minutes. Add the shallots and carrots and cook for 5 minutes more. Make a well in the center of the pan and melt the butter. Whisk the flour into the butter and cook for 1 minute, then add the wine. Remove the porcinis from the stock and stir the stock into the chicken mixture. Chop the porcinis and stir into the mixture. Thicken the sauce for 2 minutes and scoop the chicken into a 9 x 13-inch casserole or individual casseroles. Top with the potatoes, brown under the broiler for a couple of minutes, and serve.

SERVES 4

2 pounds starchy **potatoes**, peeled and cubed

Salt

½ cup **whole milk** or cream

4 stems of fresh **sage**, leaves removed and thinly sliced

Black pepper

1 cup shredded **Italian Fontina cheese**

Freshly grated **nutmeg**

1 **egg**, lightly beaten

½ ounce **dried porcini mushrooms**

2 cups **chicken stock**

2 tablespoons **EVOO** (extra-virgin olive oil)

¼ pound of ¼-inch-thick **pancetta** or prosciutto, diced

1½ pounds boneless skinless **chicken thighs** or chicken tenders, diced

3 **shallots**, chopped

2 medium **carrots**, peeled and cut into ¼-inch dice

2 tablespoons **butter**

2 tablespoons all-purpose **flour**

½ cup **dry white wine**

meatball meat loaves
with spinach-parm mashers

SERVES 4

2 pounds **starchy potatoes**, peeled and cubed

Salt

2 cups packed **farm spinach** (available in bundles rather than bags in produce section) or baby spinach

1½ cups **whole milk**

1 cup grated **Parmigiano-Reggiano** cheese, plus more for garnish

Black pepper

Freshly grated **nutmeg**

3 slices stale **bread**, torn

1½ pounds **ground beef, pork, and veal mix**

A handful of fresh **flat-leaf parsley** leaves, finely chopped

2 **garlic cloves**, finely chopped or grated

3 to 4 tablespoons grated **onion**

1 teaspoon **dried marjoram** or oregano, ⅓ palmful

2 tablespoons **EVOO** (extra-virgin olive oil)

¼ cup **tomato paste**

1 cup beef or chicken **stock**

1 (15-ounce) can petite diced or crushed **tomatoes**

A few fresh **basil leaves**, torn

Place the potatoes in a pot, cover with water, and bring to a boil. Salt the water and boil the potatoes until tender, about 15 minutes. Drain the potatoes and place them back in the hot pot with the spinach. Stir to combine, cover the pot, and let stand for 2 to 3 minutes to wilt the spinach. Add ½ cup of the milk, ⅔ cup of the cheese, and salt, pepper, and nutmeg to taste. Mash the potatoes and spinach and taste to adjust the seasoning. ■ While the potatoes come to a boil and cook, soak the bread in the remaining cup of milk. Place the meat in a bowl and add ⅓ cup cheese, the parsley, garlic, onion, marjoram or oregano, and salt and pepper. Squeeze the excess liquid from the bread and crumble it as you add it to the meat. Mix well to combine and form 4 oval loaves no more than 2 inches thick at the center. ■ Heat the EVOO in a large skillet or Dutch oven over medium-high heat. Add the meat loaves to the skillet and cook for 3 to 4 minutes on each side until lightly browned. Pull the loaves out of the pan and add the tomato paste. Stir for 1 minute, then stir the stock and tomatoes into the paste. Set the loaves back in the pan, spoon the sauce over the top, and cover with a lid to simmer for 10 minutes more, or until the loaves are cooked through. ■ Set a loaf on each plate, spoon some spinach potatoes alongside, then spoon the pan sauce over the top. Garnish with basil and the rest of the grated cheese.

sausage deconstructed:
pork & fennel one-pot

Season the pork with salt and pepper, the fennel seed, and the red pepper flakes. Dredge the pork in the flour. Heat a large skillet with 3 tablespoons of the EVOO. When the oil ripples, add the pork and brown for 5 to 6 minutes, turning once. Remove to a plate. Add the remaining tablespoon of EVOO, then add the sliced fennel, onions, garlic, and thyme. Season with salt and pepper and cook to soften, 8 to 10 minutes. Add the tomato paste and cook for 1 to 2 minutes more, then stir in the wine and scrape up the drippings. Stir in the citrus zest, juice, stock, and parsley, reduce the heat, and simmer for 5 minutes. Then add the pork and simmer for 3 to 4 minutes more. Turn off the heat and garnish with the chopped fennel fronds. Serve the pork and sauce in shallow bowls with crusty ciabatta for mopping.

SERVES 4

4 (1-inch-thick) boneless **pork loin chops**, sliced into ¼-inch-thick strips

Salt and **pepper**

1 teaspoon **fennel seed** or ground fennel or fennel pollen

1 teaspoon **crushed red pepper flakes** (optional)

¼ cup all-purpose **flour**

4 tablespoons **EVOO** (extra-virgin olive oil)

1 large **fennel bulb**, trimmed and thinly sliced, plus ¼ cup fennel fronds, chopped for garnish

1 **onion**, thinly sliced

3 to 4 **garlic cloves**, grated or finely chopped

2 tablespoons chopped fresh **thyme leaves**

3 tablespoons **tomato paste**

1 cup dry white or red **wine**

1 teaspoon orange or lemon **zest** plus 2 tablespoons **juice**

1 cup **chicken stock**

¼ cup fresh **flat-leaf parsley** leaves, chopped

1 loaf **ciabatta bread**, cut into chunks and toasted

individual vegetable potpies

1 sheet **prepared puff pastry**, such as Dufour brand

1 **egg**, lightly beaten with a splash of water

2 tablespoons **EVOO** (extra-virgin olive oil)

4 **celery stalks** from the heart, chopped

2 medium **onions**, cut into ½-inch dice

2 medium **carrots**, peeled and cut into ½-inch dice

2 medium **parsnips**, peeled and diced

5 to 6 baby white or **Yukon Gold potatoes**, diced

1 fresh **bay leaf**

Salt and **pepper**

1 quart vegetable or chicken **stock**

3 tablespoons **butter**

3 tablespoons all-purpose **flour**

1 rounded tablespoon **Dijon mustard**

1 cup **frozen peas**

3 to 4 tablespoons fresh **tarragon leaves**, chopped, or 2 tablespoons finely chopped fresh thyme leaves

Lay out the dough on a work surface. Preheat the oven to 425°F. Line a baking sheet with parchment paper. Choose the bowls that you would like to serve the potpies in; pick small, deep bowls 4 to 5 inches at the mouth. Using a small, sharp knife, cut around a bowl inverted atop the dough to make 4 disks of dough. Transfer the disks to the parchment and brush them with the egg wash. When the oven is ready, bake the disks until golden and puffed, 12 to 15 minutes. ■ Meanwhile, heat a large Dutch oven or heavy soup pot with a lid over medium heat. Add the EVOO. When the oil is hot, add the celery, onions, carrots, parsnips, potatoes, bay leaf, and salt and pepper. Stir and cover, then sweat the vegetables for 8 to 10 minutes, stirring occasionally. Add the stock and raise the heat a bit to bring the liquid to a boil. Then reduce the heat to medium-low to keep a rolling simmer. Melt the butter in a microwave or small pot and combine with the flour and mustard. Stir the roux into the broth and thicken to gravy consistency, 1 to 2 minutes. Stir the peas and tarragon or thyme into the vegetables and remove the bay leaf. ■ Ladle the vegetable mixture into individual bowls and top with rounds of crispy dough.

halibut with blct: bacon, leeks & cherry tomatoes

2 **leeks**

4 **halibut fillets**, 6 ounces each

Salt and **pepper**

¼ cup all-purpose **flour** or cornmeal

1 tablespoon **Old Bay seafood seasoning**

1 tablespoon **EVOO** (extra-virgin olive oil)

4 slices **bacon**, chopped

1 pint **cherry tomatoes**, halved

2 tablespoons **butter**, softened

1 teaspoon **hot sauce**

2 sandwich-size **English muffins**

Trim the leeks of tough tops, 4 to 5 inches, and trim the root ends. Halve the leeks lengthwise. Slice them and wash vigorously in a large bowl of water, then drain on a clean dish towel. ■ Pat the fish dry and season with salt and pepper. Mix the flour or cornmeal with the Old Bay seasoning, then pat the top of the fillets in the mixture. Heat the EVOO in a large skillet over medium-high heat. Add the fish crusted side down. Cook for 5 to 6 minutes, turn, and cook for 2 minutes more. Then remove the fish to a platter and tent loosely with foil. Add the bacon to the pan and brown for 3 to 4 minutes. Add the leeks and wilt for 2 minutes, then add the tomatoes, heat them through, and turn off the heat. ■ Meanwhile, in a small bowl combine the butter and hot sauce. Toast the English muffins and spread with the butter mixture. Halve the English muffins, making 8 half-moons, total. ■ Pour the leeks and tomatoes over the fish. Serve 2 half-moon buttered muffins alongside.

tilapia piccata

Salt

½ pound **thin spaghetti** or angel hair pasta

4 small **tilapia fillets**

Black pepper

All-purpose **flour**, for dredging

3 tablespoons **EVOO** (extra-virgin olive oil)

2 **garlic cloves**, crushed

⅔ to ¾ cup **dry vermouth** (eyeball it)

Juice of 2 **lemons**

½ cup fresh **flat-leaf parsley** leaves, finely chopped

3 tablespoons **capers**, drained

3 tablespoons **butter**

Serve with a steamed green vegetable, simple salad, or wilted spinach.

Bring a large pot of water to a boil for the pasta. Salt the water and cook the pasta to al dente. Heads up: Reserve about ½ cup cooking water just before draining. ■ Meanwhile, season the fish with salt and pepper and dredge lightly in flour. Heat the EVOO in a large skillet over medium heat. Add the garlic and toss in the oil for a minute or two, then add the fish and cook for 3 to 4 minutes on each side. Place on a platter and keep warm tented with foil. Add the vermouth to the skillet and remove the garlic. Stir in the lemon juice, parsley, and capers, then heat through for 30 seconds. Add the butter, melt it into the sauce, and spoon a little sauce over the fish. Toss the pasta with the reserved ½ cup cooking water and the remaining sauce in the skillet. Serve the pasta alongside the fish.

roasted red pepper & tomato soup with smoky caprese panini

SERVES 4

2 large **red bell peppers**

2 tablespoons **EVOO** (extra-virgin olive oil)

2 **garlic cloves**, chopped

1 small **carrot**, peeled and chopped

2 small **celery stalks**, chopped

1 **onion**, chopped

Salt and **pepper**

1 (28-ounce) can or 2 (15-ounce) cans **fire-roasted diced tomatoes**

2 cups chicken or vegetable **stock**

8 slices **Tuscan bread**

1-pound ball of freshly **smoked mozzarella**, cut into 16 thin slices

1 large ripe **tomato**, cut into 8 thin slices

½ cup fresh **basil leaves**

Char the peppers on all sides over an open flame on a gas stovetop or under a hot broiler (with the oven door cracked to avoid steam buildup in the oven). Place the charred peppers in a bowl, cover, and let them rest until cool enough to handle, about 10 minutes. ■ Meanwhile, heat the EVOO in a soup pot. Add the garlic, carrot, celery, and onions to the pot and season with salt and pepper. Cook to soften the vegetables for 10 minutes, then place in a food processor with the diced tomatoes. Seed and peel the peppers and add to the processor. Puree the mixture until smooth, then add back to the soup pot and stir in the stock. ■ Heat a large heavy skillet or panini press. Make sandwiches with 2 slices of cheese on each slice of bread and 2 slices of ripe tomato per sandwich, seasoned with salt and pepper and some torn basil. Stack the sammies together and add to the hot skillet or press. If using a skillet, top with a second smaller pan and weight the pan down with heavy cans. Press the sandwiches to toast and melt the cheese, a few minutes on each side or 5 minutes in a hot press. ■ Serve the soup with the sammies.

sandwich night:
the sliced chicken & mushroom rachael

A "Rachel" is a Reuben made with turkey or smoked turkey rather than corned beef. This sammie, The Rachael, swaps thinly sliced, freshly cooked chicken breast for the turkey—and it combines sweet sautéed onions with the sauerkraut, swaps nutty Gruyère for deli Swiss cheese, and adds homemade herbed Thousand Island dressing and sautéed mushrooms to complement the cheese and chicken, to boot.

In a small skillet, melt 2 tablespoons of the butter over medium heat, add the mushrooms, and raise the heat a bit. Cook the mushrooms for 8 to 10 minutes until tender and dark. Add the sage midway through the cooking time. Season the mushrooms with salt and pepper after they're dark and tender, as salt slows the browning by drawing out liquids. ■ Meanwhile, in a second small skillet over medium heat melt another tablespoon of butter. Add the onions, season with salt and pepper, and cook until tender, 10 to 12 minutes. Stir in the sauerkraut, warm through, and turn off the heat. ■ While the onions cook, heat a cast-iron pan or griddle to medium-high heat. Season the chicken liberally with Montreal Steak Seasoning. Add the EVOO to the pan or griddle and cook the chicken, turning once, for 12 minutes, or until done. Remove from the heat and wipe down the skillet or griddle, and lower the heat to medium-low. Slice the chicken thin on an angle. ■ While the chicken cooks, stir the sour cream, relish, and ketchup together in a small bowl and season with the fresh herbs. ■ Lightly butter one side of the slices of bread with the remaining tablespoon of butter. Build the sandwiches with buttered sides facing out, in this order: dressing, cheese, mushrooms, sliced chicken, sauerkraut with onions, cheese, and ending with the dressing to set in place. Grill the sandwiches for about 3 minutes on each side. Serve with the pickles and salted radishes.

SERVES 4

4 tablespoons (½ stick) **butter**

½ pound **baby portabella mushrooms**, sliced

2 tablespoons fresh **sage leaves**, thinly sliced, or 1½ teaspoons dried sage

Salt and **pepper**

1 large **onion**, thinly sliced

1-pound package **sauerkraut**, rinsed and drained

4 boneless skinless **chicken breast** halves, 6 ounces each

McCormick Montreal Steak Seasoning or other grill seasoning blend

1 tablespoon **EVOO** (extra-virgin olive oil)

½ cup **sour cream**

2 tablespoons **dill relish**

3 tablespoons **ketchup**

2 tablespoons chopped fresh **dill** or 1½ teaspoons dried dill

2 tablespoons chopped fresh **flat-leaf parsley** leaves

8 slices marble rye, rye, or pumpernickel **bread**

8 slices **Gruyère** or deli Swiss cheese

4 large **deli pickles**

1 bunch of **radishes**, halved and salted

green bean & bass pouches

SERVES 4

1 pound trimmed fresh **green beans**

1 small **red bell pepper**, seeded and sliced

2 **baby bok choy**, sliced lengthwise

12 thin slices of peeled fresh **gingerroot**

1 teaspoon **ground coriander**, ⅓ palmful

2 teaspoons **Old Bay seafood seasoning**, ⅔ palmful

Black pepper

4 (6- to 8-ounce) **black bass** or sea bass fillets

½ cup **hoisin sauce**

¼ cup **orange juice**

2 **scallions**, finely chopped

2 tablespoons fresh **cilantro leaves**, chopped

Preheat the oven to 425°F. ■ Cut off 4 large rectangles of foil, 16 to 18 inches each. Place a piece of the foil on a baking sheet and spread the other 3 across the countertop. Scatter one quarter of the beans, peppers, and bok choy in the center of each piece of foil. Arrange 3 slices of ginger on top of each vegetable stack. Combine the coriander, Old Bay, and a few grinds of black pepper, then sprinkle the mixture over the top of the fish. Arrange the fillets over the vegetables. ■ In a small bowl combine the hoisin with the orange juice, then drizzle the sauce evenly over the fish. Scatter the scallions and cilantro over the fish and fold the long sides of foil up over the fish. Roll down a few turns to secure, then roll in the short sides to secure. Once the packets are formed you should be able to line up the four packets on a large baking sheet. Bake for 15 minutes, or until the fish is just opaque (open one packet to check); transfer the pouches onto plates, open the pouches, and serve.

teriyaki noodles

SERVES 4

Salt

1 pound **whole-wheat spaghetti**

3 tablespoons high-temperature cooking **oil**, such as canola, sunflower, or peanut

¾ pound **flank steak**, patted dry and thinly sliced on an angle

Coarse black pepper

1 bunch of **scallions**, cleaned and trimmed of root end and rough tops, sliced on an angle

1 cup frozen shelled **edamame**, defrosted

2 inches of fresh **gingerroot**, peeled and grated or finely chopped

3 to 4 **garlic cloves**, grated or chopped

⅓ cup **teriyaki sauce**

Bring a large pot of water to a boil, salt the water, and cook the pasta to al dente. Drain the pasta. ■ Heat the oil in a skillet or wok over high heat. Add the meat and stir-fry for a couple minutes. Add a liberal amount of coarse black pepper, the scallions, edamame, ginger, and garlic, then stir-fry for 2 minutes more and stir in the sauce. Toss the stir-fry with the noodles and serve.

spanish chicken stew
with manchego polenta

Heat the EVOO in a cast-iron skillet or large pan over medium heat. Season the chicken thighs with salt, pepper, and the paprika. Brown the chicken for a couple minutes on each side, then add the chorizo and brown for a couple minutes. Add the onions and garlic and cook for 5 minutes more. Add the wine to deglaze the pan, then add the tomatoes, piquillos, and parsley. Reduce the heat to a simmer. ■ In a medium pot, bring the stock to a boil. Whisk in the polenta and stir to thicken, 2 to 3 minutes. Stir the butter and cheese into the polenta, then spoon into shallow bowls and make a well in the center. Fill the polenta-lined bowls with stew and serve.

SERVES 4

1 tablespoon **EVOO** (extra-virgin olive oil)

1 pound boneless skinless **chicken thighs**, trimmed and cut into chunks

Salt and **pepper**

1½ teaspoons **paprika** or smoked paprika

½ pound **Spanish chorizo**, sliced

1 large **onion**, quartered then thinly sliced

4 **garlic cloves**, chopped

1 cup white or red Rioja **wine**

1 (28-ounce) can **stewed tomatoes**, lightly drained

½ cup **piquillo peppers**, sliced, or chopped pimientos

½ cup fresh **flat-leaf parsley** leaves, coarsely chopped

3 cups **chicken stock**

1 cup **quick-cooking polenta**

2 tablespoons **butter**

1 cup grated **manchego cheese**

italian-style monte cristo sandwiches

SERVES 4

8 slices good-quality **white bread**

½ cup fig or plum **preserves**

8 slices mild **Provolone** or Fontina cheese

8 slices **prosciutto cotto with rosemary**, such as Citterio brand

¼ cup **Dijon mustard**

3 **eggs**

½ cup **milk** or cream

½ cup grated **Parmigiano-Reggiano** cheese, a couple handfuls

¼ cup fresh **flat-leaf parsley** leaves, chopped

1 tablespoon **butter**

6 cups **arugula** or baby arugula

Juice of 1 **lemon**

2 tablespoons **EVOO** (extra-virgin olive oil), eyeball it

Salt and **pepper**

Heat a large griddle or cast-iron skillet over medium heat. ■ Prepare the sandwiches by spreading 4 slices of bread with preserves. Top each slice of bread with a slice of cheese, 2 slices of folded prosciutto, then another slice of cheese. Spread the remaining slices of bread with Dijon and set in place. ■ Beat the eggs with the milk or cream, Parm, and parsley. Nest the butter in a paper towel and wipe it across the hot pan. Dip the sandwiches into the egg mixture and griddle the sandwiches until deep golden, 3 to 4 minutes on each side. ■ Toss the arugula with the lemon juice, EVOO, and salt and pepper. ■ Cut the sandwiches from corner to corner and serve alongside the salad.

fettuccine with mushrooms

SERVES 4

Salt

1 pound **fettuccine**

1¼ pounds **mixed mushrooms**

2 to 3 **garlic cloves**, chopped

¼ cup **EVOO** (extra-virgin olive oil)

3 tablespoons chopped fresh **thyme leaves**

2 tablespoons thinly sliced fresh **sage leaves** or 2 teaspoons rubbed or ground dried sage

Black pepper

Freshly grated **nutmeg**

½ cup **Marsala** or dry white wine

½ cup **cream** or 1 cup **fresh ricotta**

A generous handful of fresh **flat-leaf parsley** leaves, finely chopped

A generous handful of grated **Pecorino Romano** cheese

Bring a large pot of water to a boil for the pasta. Add salt and cook the pasta to al dente. Heads up: Reserve a mug of cooking water just before draining. ■ Thinly slice the mushrooms, then heat the EVOO in a large skillet over medium-high heat. Add the mushrooms to the pan and sauté until deeply browned and tender, 12 to 15 minutes, adding the garlic, thyme, and sage midway. Season the tender mushrooms with salt and pepper and a little freshly grated nutmeg. Deglaze the pan with the Marsala and stir for 30 seconds. Then add the cream, or if you prefer, top the pasta with a dollop of ricotta for mixing in. Add the reserved starchy pasta cooking water—about 1 cup if using ricotta, and just enough to thin out the sauce to your liking if using cream. ■ Drain the pasta and toss with sauce, parsley, and cheese. Top with ricotta, if using, for mixing into the fettuccine as you eat.

venetian-style paella

Place the sausages in a small skillet with ¾ inch of water, bring to a boil, and par-cook for 7 to 8 minutes. ■ Meanwhile, combine the stock and saffron in a medium pot and warm. Heat a large heavy pot or deep skillet with a tight-fitting lid over medium-high heat with the EVOO. When the oil smokes, add the chicken and season liberally with salt and pepper. Brown the chicken for a couple minutes on each side, then remove to a plate. Add the par-boiled sausage and crisp up the casings, 2 to 3 minutes, then remove and cut into large chunks. Add the butter to the pot and melt. ■ Add the pasta and toast for a couple minutes, then add the onions and garlic. Season the pasta with salt and pepper, then add the bay leaf and stir for 2 to 3 minutes more. Add the rice and stir to combine, then deglaze the pot with the white wine, stirring for 30 seconds. Place the chicken and sausages back into the pot, pour in the saffron stock, and stir. ■ Cover and simmer for 15 minutes. Add the seafood and tomatoes and cook for 3 to 4 minutes more, until the shrimp are opaque. If using mussels, cook until the mussels are open. Discard any that do not open. Discard the bay leaf, top with basil, and serve.

SERVES 4

1 pound hot or sweet **sausage links**

3 cups **chicken stock**

2 healthy pinches of **saffron threads**

2 tablespoons **EVOO** (extra-virgin olive oil)

6 boneless skinless **chicken thighs**, cut into large pieces

Salt and **pepper**

2 tablespoons **butter**

½ cup **orzo** pasta or broken bits of thin spaghetti

1 medium **onion**, finely chopped

4 **garlic cloves**, finely chopped

1 large fresh **bay leaf**

1¼ cups **white rice**

½ cup **dry white wine**

1 pound large deveined **shrimp** or scrubbed mussels or a combination of both

1 large ripe **tomato**, seeded and diced, or 1 (15-ounce) can diced tomatoes, drained well

1 cup loosely packed fresh **basil leaves**, torn or shredded

roasted eggplant & tomato subs

SERVES 4

¾ cup **EVOO** (extra-virgin olive oil)

2 large **garlic cloves**, crushed

2 small sprigs of fresh **rosemary**

½ teaspoon **crushed red pepper flakes**

2 small or medium **eggplants**, about 1½ pounds

2 large **tomatoes**

Salt and **pepper**

1 cup packed fresh **basil leaves**

½ cup packed fresh **flat-leaf parsley** leaves

¼ cup **shelled pistachios**, toasted

A couple handfuls of grated **Parmigiano-Reggiano** cheese

2 cups **arugula leaves**

4 sesame **sub rolls**, split lengthwise

12 thin slices smoked fresh **mozzarella** or fresh mozzarella

Preheat the oven to 425°F. ■ In a small pot, heat about ½ cup of the EVOO with the crushed garlic, rosemary sprigs, and red pepper flakes. Let the oil infuse over low heat for a couple minutes. ■ Meanwhile, arrange cooling racks over 2 rimmed baking sheets. Trim the tops and bottoms of the eggplants and thinly slice the eggplants and tomatoes. Brush the eggplant with seasoned oil using a pastry brush and arrange the slices on a rack over one baking sheet. Arrange the sliced tomatoes on the other rack and sheet and season both with salt and pepper. Roast for 15 minutes, or until the eggplant is tender and slightly shriveled up. ■ While the eggplant and tomatoes roast, combine the basil, parsley, nuts, Parmigiano, and salt and pepper in a food processor and pulse to finely chop. Then stream in about ¼ cup of EVOO to form a thick pesto. ■ Arrange about ½ cup of arugula leaves on each sub roll bottom. Top with layered slices of roasted eggplant, mozzarella, and roasted tomatoes. Spread pesto on the roll tops and set in place. Halve the sammies and serve.

mini sausage meatball minestra

SERVES 4

1¼ pounds bulk **sweet Italian sausage**

3 tablespoons **EVOO** (extra-virgin olive oil)

1 **onion**, chopped

3 to 4 **garlic cloves**, chopped

2 large heads of **escarole**, trimmed, washed, and chopped

Salt and **pepper**

Freshly grated **nutmeg**

1 (15-ounce) can **cannellini beans**, drained

2 quarts **chicken stock**

2 cups **short cut pasta** such as mini penne or ditalini

Grated **Pecorino Romano** cheese

Crusty bread

Heat 1 tablespoon of the EVOO in a large skillet. Roll the sausage into walnut-sized meatballs. Drop them into the skillet and brown on all sides, then remove. Heat the remaining 2 tablespoons EVOO in a large pot over medium heat. Sauté the onions and garlic for 5 minutes, then wilt in the escarole and season with salt, pepper, and nutmeg. Add the beans and heat through. Stir in the stock and bring to a boil, then add the pasta and cook to al dente. Add the meatballs back to the pot for the last 4 minutes of cooking. Adjust the seasonings and serve with cheese sprinkled heavily on top. Pass the crusty bread for mopping.

lamb chops with pomegranate sauce & saffron pilaf

Store-bought pomegranate juice can be used when fresh are not in season.

Preheat the broiler and arrange the rack 8 inches from the broiler. ■ Heat a pot with a tight-fitting lid over medium heat. Add the butter and melt, then add the orzo and stir. Toast the pasta to golden brown, 3 minutes, then add the rice and stir to combine. Add the saffron threads to the pan and stir in the stock. Bring the liquid to a boil, then reduce to a simmer and cover the pot. Cook the rice for 15 to 18 minutes, until tender. ■ Meanwhile, roll the pomegranate on the counter while applying pressure for a minute. Hold the pomegranate over a small pot and cut into it with a small sharp knife; the juice will come rushing out. Squeeze the pomegranate until ¾ to 1 cup of juice is produced. Add the wine and Worcestershire to the juice, then add the peppercorns, cloves, and bay leaf. Bring to a boil, reduce the heat to a simmer and reduce the liquid by half, 6 minutes or so. Pour a little sauce into a small bowl, stir in the cornstarch, and then pour the mixture back into the sauce. Cook to thicken, about 1 minute; remove the whole cloves and bay leaf before serving. ■ Arrange the chops on a broiler pan and season with salt and pepper. Broil for 3 to 4 minutes, or only 1 minute on each side for pink centers. ■ When the chops go in, heat the EVOO in a medium skillet over medium heat. Add the garlic and stir for 2 minutes, then wilt in the spinach and season with salt, pepper, and nutmeg. ■ Serve the chops topped with pomegranate sauce, and with saffron pilaf and wilted spinach alongside.

SERVES 4

- 2 tablespoons **butter**
- ¼ cup **orzo pasta**
- 1 cup **white rice**
- 2 pinches of **saffron threads**
- 1¾ cups **chicken stock**
- 1 to 2 large **pomegranates** or 1 cup store-bought pomegranate juice
- ½ cup **red wine**
- 2 tablespoons **Worcestershire sauce**
- 6 **peppercorns**
- 3 whole **cloves**
- 1 fresh **bay leaf**
- 1½ tablespoons **cornstarch**
- 12 rib **lamb chops**
- **Salt** and **pepper**
- 2 tablespoons **EVOO** (extra-virgin olive oil)
- 2 large **garlic cloves**, chopped
- 1 pound farm **spinach** (available in bundles rather than bags in produce section), washed and dried
- Freshly grated **nutmeg**

three-pepper & onion spaghetti

Salt

1 pound **spaghetti**

3 tablespoons **EVOO** (extra-virgin olive oil)

1½ teaspoons **fennel seed**, ½ palmful

1 large **red bell pepper**, quartered lengthwise, seeded, and thinly sliced

2 **cubanelle peppers**, halved lengthwise, seeded, and thinly sliced

1 **red chile pepper**, seeded and thinly sliced, or 1 teaspoon crushed red pepper flakes

1 large **onion** or red onion, quartered lengthwise and thinly sliced

3 to 4 **garlic cloves**, chopped

Black pepper

½ cup **dry white wine**

½ cup chicken or vegetable **stock**

1 (28-ounce) can **crushed Italian tomatoes**

2 tablespoons **butter**, cut into small pieces

Grated **Parmigiano-Reggiano** cheese

½ cup fresh **basil leaves**, shredded or torn

Bring a large pot of water to a boil, salt the water, and cook the pasta to al dente. ■ While the water comes to a boil, heat the EVOO in a large skillet over medium-high heat. Add the fennel seed and stir for 1 minute, then add all the peppers and onions as you chop. Sauté for 8 to 10 minutes, then add the garlic as you chop and season with salt and pepper. When the peppers and onions are tender, add the wine and stir for 30 seconds, then add the stock and tomatoes. Reduce the sauce for 7 to 8 minutes more while you cook the pasta. ■ Drain the pasta, drop it into the skillet, and toss it with the butter and the sauce. Sprinkle in a little cheese, top with the basil, and serve immediately.

braised wurst sausages
with cabbage, red onion, & apple slaw

Place the sausages in a skillet and add ½ inch of water and a drizzle of oil. Bring to a boil, then reduce the heat to medium and allow the liquid to evaporate, cooking the sausages through. Once the liquid evaporates, the oil will help brown and crisp up the casings. ■ Meanwhile, combine the vinegar, sugar, peppercorns, cloves, bay leaves, and sea salt in a small pot. Bring to a boil, stir, then reduce for 5 to 6 minutes over medium-low heat. ■ While the brine reduces, combine the cabbage, red onions, and apples in a bowl. Sprinkle with caraway or cumin seed if you like the flavor. ■ Pour the hot reduced brine through a strainer over the cabbage mix in a slow stream. Evenly distribute it, then pour about ¼ cup of oil over the salad. Season with salt and pepper, toss to combine, and adjust the seasoning. ■ Toast the bread. In a small bowl, combine the softened butter with the herbs. Spread the mixture on the warm toast. ■ Serve the sausages with the toast, slaw salad, mustard, radishes, and pickles.

SERVES 4

8 links good-quality **bratwurst**, bockwurst, weisswurst, or knackwurst sausages

A drizzle plus ¼ cup olive or vegetable **oil**

1 cup **white wine vinegar** or cider vinegar

¼ to ⅓ cup **sugar** (eyeball it)

8 **peppercorns**

2 to 3 whole **cloves**

2 fresh **bay leaves**

1 teaspoon **sea salt** or kosher salt

1 small head of **red cabbage** or ½ medium head, cored and thinly shredded, 1 pound

1 medium **red onion**, peeled, halved, and thinly sliced

1 **green apple**, quartered, cored, and thinly sliced

1 teaspoon **caraway seed** or cumin seed (optional)

Salt and **pepper**

4 slices **pumpernickel bread**

8 tablespoons (1 stick) **butter**, softened

¼ cup finely chopped fresh **herbs** such as chives, dill, or flat-leaf parsley

1 cup good-quality **spicy mustard**

Fresh **radishes**, trimmed and lightly salted

Cornichons or baby gherkin pickles

baked shells

Salt

1 pound medium or large **shell pasta** (not stuffing shells)

2 tablespoons **EVOO** (extra-virgin olive oil)

1 **onion**, chopped

2 to 3 **garlic cloves**, finely chopped

1 (10-ounce) box **frozen chopped spinach**, defrosted and wrung dry in a clean kitchen towel

Freshly grated **nutmeg**

Black pepper

2 tablespoons **butter**

1 (28-ounce) can **Italian tomatoes**

½ cup fresh **basil leaves**, 10 to 12 leaves

1 cup **ricotta cheese**

1 cup **Parmigiano-Reggiano** cheese

½-pound ball of **fresh mozzarella** cheese, cut into ½-inch dice

Preheat the oven to 400°F. ■ Bring a large pot of water to a boil for the pasta. Salt the water and cook the shells for 2 to 3 minutes less than the package directions. Heads up: You will need to reserve ½ cup starchy cooking water just before draining the pasta. ■ Meanwhile, heat a medium-size pot or high-sided skillet over medium heat with the EVOO. Add the onions and garlic and sauté for 3 to 4 minutes. Add the spinach, pulling it apart as you add it, and season with a little freshly grated nutmeg, salt, and pepper. When the spinach mixture is warm through, transfer it to a small dish and reserve. Return the pot to the heat, add the butter, and melt. Add the tomatoes and break up with a spoon. Season with salt and pepper, add the basil leaves, and cook to thicken the sauce, 7 to 8 minutes. ■ Drain the pasta and return the pasta to the hot pot. To the pasta, add the spinach, reserved starchy water, ricotta cheese, and half of the Parmigiano-Reggiano. Adjust the salt and pepper and transfer to a baking dish. Top the pasta mixture with the tomato sauce, mozzarella, and remaining Parmigiano. Bake until the cheeses are melted and bubbly, 6 to 8 minutes.

drunken spaghetti
with black kale

1 bottle **dry Italian red wine**

Salt

1 pound **spaghetti**

3 tablespoons **EVOO** (extra-virgin olive oil)

¼ pound **pancetta**, smoked pancetta, or speck, chopped into fine dice

4 **garlic cloves**, finely chopped

2 bundles of black, Tuscan, or Dinosaur **kale**, thinly sliced

Black pepper

Freshly grated **nutmeg**

½ cup grated **Pecorino Romano** cheese, plus some to shave at table

Pour the whole bottle of wine into a pasta pot and add about the same amount of water. Bring to a boil, salt the liquids, and cook the pasta to just shy of al dente. Heads up: reserve a cup of starchy cooking liquid just before draining. ■ Meanwhile, heat a deep skillet over medium to medium-high heat with the EVOO. Add the pancetta and crisp, 2 to 3 minutes, then add the garlic and swirl around for 2 minutes more. Add the kale and wilt into the pan and then season with salt, pepper, and nutmeg to taste. Add the starchy cooking liquid and drained pasta and the grated cheese. Toss vigorously for at least a full minute, then serve in shallow bowls. Pass the pecorino to shave over the pasta at the table.

leeky chicken soup

To clean leeks, chop them first and then wash them. Trim the tough tops and root ends, halve them lengthwise, then slice them ½ inch thick. Fill a large bowl or sink with water, add the leeks, and separate the slices to let the grit fall away. Remove the leeks with a skimmer and dry in a salad spinner or on a clean kitchen towel.

Place the chicken and bay leaf in a small pan and add water almost to cover. Place over high heat, bring to a boil, reduce to a simmer, and poach the chicken until cooked through, about 10 minutes. ■ Meanwhile, heat the EVOO in a soup pot or Dutch oven over medium heat. Add the leeks and garlic, season with salt and pepper, then stir, cover, and cook for 7 to 8 minutes. Add the wine and cook out for 1 minute, then add the stock and bring to a boil. Reduce the heat to a simmer. Remove the chicken from the poaching liquid and dice, then stir into the stock. Strain the poaching liquid and add it to the soup. Add the egg pasta, thyme, and lemon zest. Cook at a low boil until the pasta is tender. Stir in the parsley and adjust the salt and pepper. Serve with crusty bread spread with soft cheese.

SERVES 4

2 boneless skinless **chicken breast** halves

1 large **bay leaf**, fresh or dried

2 tablespoons **EVOO** (extra-virgin olive oil)

4 large **leeks**, trimmed, washed, and dried

3 to 4 **garlic cloves**, chopped

Salt and **pepper**

1 cup **dry white wine**

1 quart **chicken stock**

2 cups **egg pasta**, such as broken egg fettuccine or tagliatelle

2 tablespoons fresh **thyme leaves**, chopped

2 teaspoons grated **lemon zest**

¼ cup fresh **flat-leaf parsley** leaves, chopped

Crusty baguette, sliced

Soft **cheese** such as goat cheese, robiola, Camembert, or Boursin

lick your chops supper

SERVES 4

3 large **potatoes**, peeled and cubed

2 large **parsnips** or parsley root, peeled and chopped

Salt

½ to ⅔ cup **whole milk**

Black pepper

Freshly grated **nutmeg**

1 cup shredded **Italian Fontina** or ¾ cup crumbled Gorgonzola cheese

4 large bone-in **pork or veal chops**, about 1½-to-2 inches thick

1 small bundle of fresh **sage leaves**, chopped

3 tablespoons **EVOO** (extra-virgin olive oil)

2 large **garlic cloves**, crushed

½ cup **dry vermouth** or ¾ cup dry white wine

1 pound trimmed **broccolini spears**

2 tablespoons **butter**

Preheat the oven to 375°F. ■ Place the potatoes and parsnips in a medium pot and cover with water. Bring to a boil, salt the water, and cook until tender, 15 to 18 minutes. Drain and place back in the hot pot. Mash with the milk and salt, pepper, and nutmeg to taste. Stir in the cheese to melt. ■ While the potatoes and parsnips come to a boil, rub the chops with lots of salt, pepper, and sage. Once the potatoes are boiling, heat the EVOO over medium heat in a large oven-safe skillet. Add the garlic and sauté for 3 minutes, then remove the garlic with a slotted spoon and raise the heat to medium-high. ■ Add the chops and brown on both sides and along the edges, 5 to 6 minutes. Add the vermouth or wine to the pan and transfer to the oven. Cook the meat through for 7 to 8 minutes more. ■ While the meat cooks, bring a couple of inches of water to a boil and salt the water. Cook the broccolini for 5 to 6 minutes, then drain. ■ Remove the chops to 4 plates. Add the butter to the pan and whisk into the pan juices, then spoon the sauce over the chops. Serve with the mashed potatoes and parsnips and the broccolini alongside.

white meat sauce
with pappardelle

Heat a heavy sauce pot over medium-high heat with the EVOO. Add the pancetta and brown for 2 to 3 minutes, then add the meat and lightly brown, 3 to 4 minutes more. Add the carrot, onions, and garlic and season with salt and pepper. Cook for 5 minutes to soften the vegetables, then stir in the spinach and season with nutmeg. Stir in the tomato paste for 1 minute. Add the wine and reduce for 30 seconds, then add the stock and bring to a boil. Add the milk, reduce the heat, and simmer for 10 to 2 minutes. ■ Meanwhile, bring a large pot of water to a boil for the pasta. Salt the water and cook the pasta to al dente. Reserve a little of the starchy cooking water. Drain the pasta and toss with the starchy water, the meat sauce, and some cheese. Toss for at least a full minute to combine. Serve with more grated cheese on top.

SERVES 4

2 tablespoons **EVOO** (extra-virgin olive oil)

¼ pound **pancetta**, chopped into fine dice

1 pound **ground veal** or ground pork

1 **carrot**, finely chopped or grated

1 **onion**, finely chopped

2 large **garlic cloves**, chopped

Salt and **pepper**

1 (10-ounce) box **frozen chopped spinach**, defrosted and wrung dry in a clean kitchen towel

Freshly grated **nutmeg**, about ¼ teaspoon

2 tablespoons **tomato paste**

½ cup **dry white wine**

2 cups **chicken stock**

½ cup **whole milk**

1 pound **pappardelle**, tagliatelle, or fettuccine pasta

Grated **Parmigiano-Reggiano** cheese

poached salmon, creamy dill mushrooms & pan-tatoes with shallots & watercress

4 (6- to 8-ounce) skinless **salmon fillets**

1 **bay leaf**

1 small bunch fresh **dill**, stems removed and reserved, leaves chopped

3 tablespoons **EVOO** (extra-virgin olive oil)

8 to 10 small **Yukon Gold potatoes**, very thinly sliced

Salt and **pepper**

2 large **shallots**, thinly sliced

2 bundles of **watercress**, trimmed

2 tablespoons **butter**

1 **leek**, trimmed, halved lengthwise, thinly sliced, washed, and dried

½ pound **mushroom caps**, thinly sliced

½ cup **dry white wine**

½ cup **chicken stock**

⅓ cup **sour cream**

Place the salmon in a small pan with the bay leaf and dill stems and add water to come to the top of the fillets, but do not cover them. Bring the water to a boil, then reduce the heat to a simmer and gently cook for 10 minutes until firm and opaque. ■ Place a nonstick skillet over medium-high heat with the EVOO. Add the potatoes in an even layer, season with salt and pepper, and begin to brown, 3 to 4 minutes. Add the shallots and continue to cook, turning occasionally, for 7 to 8 minutes more. Wilt in the watercress and combine it with the potatoes and shallots. ■ Meanwhile, melt the butter in small pan over medium heat. Add the leeks and mushrooms and gently cook until very tender, about 10 minutes. Season the leeks and mushrooms with salt and pepper. Raise the heat a bit and add the wine. Reduce for 30 seconds, add the stock, and swirl in the sour cream and chopped dill. Turn off the heat. ■ Serve the poached salmon with the creamy mushroom sauce on top, and with potatoes and watercress alongside.

chicken paillards with wilted greens & white beans & gremolata bread crumbs

Cut into and across the chicken breast pieces and open them up like a book. Pound between 2 sheets of wax paper to ¼-inch thickness, then season with salt and pepper and reserve. ■ Heat 4 tablespoons of the EVOO in a large skillet over medium-low heat with the anchovies, if using. Melt the anchovies into the oil until they dissolve, then add half of the garlic and stir for 2 minutes. Add the bread crumbs and stir and cook until deeply golden in color. Stir in the lemon zest, parsley, and red pepper flakes. Transfer the bread crumbs to a bowl. ■ Wipe out the pan and return it to the stove. Heat ½ tablespoon of the EVOO. Cook 2 pieces of chicken for 5 to 6 minutes, turning once, then transfer to a plate and cover with foil to keep warm. Repeat the process. Once cooked, remove the remaining chicken to the plate and add the remaining tablespoon of EVOO to the pan. Add the remaining garlic to the pan and sauté for a minute or two, then wilt in the escarole. Season the greens with salt, pepper, and the nutmeg. Once the escarole is wilted, stir in the stock and add the beans to heat through, about 2 minutes. ■ Serve each paillard on a dinner plate topped with a generous mound of greens and beans and a healthy sprinkle of flavored bread crumbs.

SERVES 2

2 boneless skinless **chicken breast** halves, 6 ounces each

Salt and **pepper**

6 tablespoons **EVOO** (extra-virgin olive oil)

6 flat **anchovy fillets** (optional)

6 **garlic cloves**, finely chopped

1 cup **bread crumbs**

Zest of 2 **lemons**

½ cup fresh **flat-leaf parsley** leaves, finely chopped

2 pinches of **crushed red pepper flakes**

1 medium head of **escarole**, trimmed, washed, and dried

⅛ teaspoon freshly grated **nutmeg**

½ cup **chicken stock**

1 can **cannellini beans**, rinsed and drained

steak with salsa verde & potato & bitter green hash

SERVES 4

4 (6- to 8-ounce) **flatiron steaks**, or 4 (8-ounce) strip steaks

Salt and **pepper**

⅓ to ½ cup **EVOO** (extra-virgin olive oil)

1 large **shallot**, roughly chopped

2 **garlic cloves**, 1 clove grated or finely chopped and 1 clove crushed

2 **flat anchovy fillets**

1 cup fresh **flat-leaf parsley** leaves, loosely packed

2 to 3 sprigs fresh **rosemary**, leaves removed from stems

A small handful of fresh **sage leaves**, coarsely chopped

½ teaspoon **crushed red pepper flakes** (eyeball it)

3 tablespoons **Worcestershire sauce**

8 thinly sliced baby **Yukon Gold potatoes**

4 cups chopped **arugula**, watercress, and/or escarole

Freshly grated **nutmeg**

Heat a cast-iron skillet or a large grill pan to high heat. ■ Season the meat with salt and pepper, drizzle with EVOO, and bring to room temperature. ■ To a food processor bowl add the shallot, the grated or finely chopped garlic, the anchovies, parsley, rosemary, sage, red pepper flakes, lots of black pepper, a little salt, and the Worcestershire sauce plus about ¼ cup EVOO. Pulse to chop the ingredients into a thick green sauce, then transfer to a bowl. ■ Heat 2 tablespoons of the EVOO in a large nonstick skillet over medium heat with the crushed garlic. Remove the garlic and add the potatoes in an even layer, season with salt and pepper, and cook to brown, 3 to 4 minutes on the first side. Turn and cook for 3 to 4 minutes more, then add the greens to the pan and season with a little nutmeg. Turn off the heat. ■ While the potatoes cook, throw the steaks into the hot skillet and cook for 7 to 8 minutes total for pink centers and up to 12 minutes for medium-well, turning once. ■ Serve the steaks with the salsa verde on top and the potato-greens hash on the side.

mini meatballs
with orecchiette

Preheat the oven to 425°F. ■ In a small bowl, combine the bread crumbs with the cheese and nutmeg, then add the milk to barely dampen the crumbs, working the moisture through with your fingertips. ■ Place the meat in a mixing bowl and add salt and pepper, the crumb mixture, parsley, and egg. Cover a baking sheet with parchment paper and grab a small scooper if you'd like extra help rolling meatballs. Roll the balls into the size of walnuts and drizzle them with some EVOO. Roast for 10 to 12 minutes to cook through. ■ Bring a large pot of water to a boil for the pasta. When the water boils, salt it and cook the pasta to al dente. ■ Meanwhile, heat a sauce pot or Dutch oven over medium heat with the 2 tablespoons of EVOO. Add the garlic and onions and cook gently for 5 to 6 minutes to soften. Add the wine and stir for 30 seconds, then add the stock and tomatoes. Season with salt and a little pepper and simmer for 10 minutes to thicken. Stir in the basil. ■ Drain the pasta and toss with the butter, a handful of cheese, and a few ladles of sauce. Add the meatballs to the remaining sauce and turn to coat. Serve the pasta in shallow bowls with mini meatballs on top. Pass the grated cheese at the table.

SERVES 4 TO 6

½ cup **bread crumbs**, a couple handfuls

¼ to ⅓ cup grated **Parmigiano-Reggiano** cheese, a generous handful, plus a handful to toss with the pasta and some to pass at the table

⅛ teaspoon freshly grated **nutmeg**

3 to 5 tablespoons **whole milk**

1 pound **ground beef, pork, and veal mix** or ground veal

Salt and **pepper**

¼ cup fresh **flat-leaf parsley** leaves, finely chopped

1 **egg**

EVOO (extra-virgin olive oil) for liberal drizzling, plus 2 tablespoons

1 pound **orecchiette pasta** or other short cut pasta

2 **garlic cloves**, finely chopped

1 small **onion**, finely chopped

½ cup **dry white wine**

½ cup **chicken stock**

1 (28-ounce) can **Italian crushed tomatoes**

½ cup fresh **basil leaves**, torn or shredded

2 tablespoons **butter**, cut into small pieces

5 yes! the kids will eat it

Yum-o! Yes, your kids will eat it! Here are a dozen delicious, nutritious, and cost-friendly meals that are designed to bring the family not only to the table for dinner but to the kitchen for its preparation as well. Kids who help prepare meals are personally vested in them and are much less likely to be picky eaters because of it. Being able to cook for yourself improves your health and the overall quality of your life. When times were tough in my own life, being able to provide good food for myself sustained me emotionally as well as practically. Eat well. Eat together. Yum-o!

Yum-o! is Rachael Ray's nonprofit organization that empowers kids and their families to develop healthy relationships with food and cooking. By providing the tools to create easy, affordable, and delicious meals, Yum-o! is changing the way America eats. For more information about the Yum-o! organization, please visit *www.yum-o.org*.

tuna & white bean pasta
with gremolata bread crumbs

For homemade bread crumbs, keep leftover slices or ends of bread in the fridge or freezer until you have a few cupfuls. Toast the bread, then process it into crumbs. Store in a sealed container or plastic bag in the freezer.

Heat 4 tablespoons of the EVOO in a small pan over medium-low heat with the anchovies, if using. Melt the anchovies into the oil until they dissolve, then add 4 cloves of the garlic and stir for 2 minutes. Add the bread crumbs and cook, stirring, until deeply golden in color. Stir in the lemon zest, the parsley, and the red pepper flakes. Turn off the heat and transfer the gremolata bread crumbs to a bowl.
■ Bring a large pot of water to a boil for the pasta. When the water boils, season with salt, add the pasta, and cook to al dente. Heads up: You will need to reserve a ladle of the pasta cooking water before draining. ■ Heat a large skillet over medium heat with the remaining 2 tablespoons of EVOO. Add the celery, onions, and the remaining 2 cloves of garlic to the pan and cook until just tender, about 5 minutes. Add the white beans and rosemary and heat through for 2 to 3 minutes more. Add the wine, tuna, and tomato, if using. Stir for 2 minutes and then turn off the heat. ■ Add the reserved ladle of starchy cooking water to the skillet along with the drained pasta, then toss to combine. Serve in shallow bowls with lots of gremolata bread crumbs and a drizzle of oil on top.

SERVES 4

6 tablespoons **EVOO** (extra-virgin olive oil), plus more for drizzling

6 flat **anchovy fillets** (optional)

6 **garlic cloves**, finely chopped

1 cup **bread crumbs**

Zest of 2 **lemons**

½ cup fresh **flat-leaf parsley** leaves, finely chopped

½ teaspoon **crushed red pepper flakes** (optional)

Salt

1 pound **penne** or ziti rigate (ridged penne or ziti pasta)

4 **celery stalks**, finely chopped

1 **red onion**, finely chopped

1 (15-ounce) can **white beans**, rinsed and drained

2 sprigs of fresh **rosemary**, leaves removed and finely chopped

½ cup **white wine**, white vermouth, or chicken stock

2 (6-ounce) cans **Italian tuna** in oil or water, drained

1 large **tomato**, seeded and chopped, or 1 (15-ounce) can diced tomatoes, drained (optional)

vegetable soup
with dumplings

SERVES 4

2 tablespoons **EVOO** (extra-virgin olive oil)

4 **celery stalks** from the heart, chopped

2 **onions**, cut into ½-inch dice

4 **carrots**, peeled and cut into ½-inch dice

1 **potato**, peeled and diced

1 **zucchini**, diced

1 fresh **bay leaf**

Salt and **pepper**

2 quarts vegetable or chicken **stock**

4 tablespoons (½ stick) **butter**

4 tablespoons all-purpose **flour**

1 rounded tablespoon **Dijon mustard**

1 (8-ounce) box **Jiffy biscuit mix**

2 tablespoons fresh **flat-leaf parsley** leaves, finely chopped

1 cup frozen **peas**

3 to 4 tablespoons fresh **tarragon leaves**, chopped

Heat a large Dutch oven or heavy soup pot with a lid over medium heat with the EVOO. When the oil is hot, add the celery, onions, carrots, potato, zucchini, bay leaf, and salt and pepper. Stir, then cover and cook for 8 to 10 minutes, stirring occasionally. Add the stock and raise the heat to bring it to a boil. Then reduce the heat to medium-low to keep a rolling simmer. ■ Melt the butter in a microwave or small pot and combine with the flour and Dijon mustard. Whisk the roux into the soup. ■ Prepare the biscuit mix according to the package directions, adding the parsley to the dough. ■ Stir the peas and tarragon into the soup. Use 2 teaspoons to drop walnut-size dumplings into the soup and cover the pot with the lid. Cook for 6 minutes, then uncover and check that the dumplings are firm. Discard the bay leaf. Ladle the soup into bowls and serve immediately.

quick rosemary chicken & potatoes

SERVES 4

1 pound baby **Yukon Gold potatoes**

1 small head of **cauliflower**, cut into florets

8 **garlic cloves**, smashed and peeled

Salt and **pepper**

1 cup **chicken stock**

8 bone-in, skin-on **chicken thighs**

4 sprigs of fresh **rosemary**, leaves removed and finely chopped

2 tablespoons **EVOO** (extra-virgin olive oil)

1 cup **dry white wine**

Preheat the oven to 450°F. ■ Place the potatoes, cauliflower, and garlic in a pot with a tight-fitting lid. Season with salt and pepper, add the stock, and bring to a boil. Cover and reduce the heat to a simmer, then cook for 10 to 12 minutes. ■ Meanwhile, heat a large cast-iron skillet over medium-high heat. Pat the chicken dry with a paper towel and season with salt, pepper, and rosemary. Add the EVOO to the skillet. When the oil smokes, add the chicken skin side down and cook for 10 minutes or so, turning once. ■ Remove the chicken to a plate and add the wine to the skillet, scraping up the drippings. Transfer the potatoes, cauliflower, and garlic to the skillet with a slotted spoon, and top with the browned chicken. Transfer to the oven and roast for 10 to 12 minutes more, until the vegetables are very tender and the chicken is cooked through. ■ Serve hot from the pan.

sticky orange chicken

SERVES 4

2 pounds **sweet potatoes**, peeled and cubed

Salt

1 cup warm **apple cider**

½ cup **cream**

Pinch of ground **cinnamon**

Freshly grated **nutmeg**

Black pepper

2 tablespoons **EVOO** (extra-virgin olive oil)

4 boneless skinless **chicken breast** halves or 8 boneless skinless chicken thighs

2 tablespoons **cider vinegar**

⅓ cup **orange marmalade**

1½ cups **chicken stock**

1 tablespoon fresh **rosemary leaves**, finely chopped

2 tablespoons fresh **thyme leaves**, finely chopped

Place the potatoes in a pot, cover with water, and bring to a boil. Salt the water and cook the potatoes until tender, 15 to 18 minutes; once tender, drain and return to the hot pot. Mash with the cider and cream, then season with cinnamon, nutmeg, salt, and pepper. ■ While the potatoes cook, heat the EVOO in a cast-iron or stainless steel skillet. Add the chicken to the hot pan and cook for 10 minutes, turning once. Transfer the chicken to a plate and deglaze the pan with the vinegar. Whisk in the marmalade, stock, and herbs. Add the chicken back to the skillet and turn it in the sauce to coat. Let the sauce thicken for 1 to 2 minutes, then serve the chicken and sauce with mashed sweet potatoes alongside.

turkey meat loaves with
smashed sweet potatoes &
peas & radishes

SERVES 6

5 medium **sweet potatoes**, peeled and cubed

Salt

2 pounds **ground turkey**

2 slices **whole-wheat bread**, toasted and buttered, finely chopped

1½ cups **chicken stock**

1 **egg**, beaten

1 large **shallot**, finely chopped

2 tablespoons chopped fresh **thyme leaves**

2 rounded tablespoons **orange marmalade**

2 rounded tablespoons **grainy mustard**

Black pepper

EVOO (extra-virgin olive oil), for drizzling

4 tablespoons (½ stick) **butter**

2 tablespoons all-purpose **flour**

Splash of **orange juice**

1 tablespoon **Worcestershire sauce**

2 (10-ounce) boxes **frozen green peas**

½ cup chopped **radishes**

¼ cup chopped fresh **chives**

½ cup **cream** or half-and-half

Freshly grated **nutmeg**

Sweet potatoes are more nutrient-filled than just about any other item in the produce department. If you prefer white mashed potatoes, add peeled parsnips to the potatoes to bump up the flavor and vitamins in your mash.

Preheat the oven to 425°F. ■ Place the potatoes in a pot, cover with water, and bring to a boil; salt the water and cook until the potatoes are tender, about 12 to 15 minutes. ■ Cover a large rimmed baking sheet with parchment paper. ■ Meanwhile, mix the turkey with the bread, a splash of stock, the egg, shallots, thyme, and marmalade, then combine with the mustard and salt and pepper. Form 6 mini meat loaves and arrange on the parchment paper, drizzle with some EVOO, and roast until golden, 20 minutes or so. An instant-read thermometer inserted into the centers of the loaves should read 165°F. ■ For the gravy, over medium heat in a skillet, melt 2 tablespoons of butter, whisk in the flour for 1 minute, then whisk in a splash of orange juice, the Worcestershire, and 1 cup of the chicken stock. Cook to thicken for a few minutes and season with salt and pepper to taste. ■ To a second larger skillet, add the peas, a small splash of water, and the remaining 2 tablespoons of butter. Bring the peas to a boil, cook off the water for 2 to 3 minutes, then reduce the heat to medium and sauté with the radishes for 2 to 3 minutes more. Add the chives and season with salt and pepper. ■ Drain the cooked sweet potatoes and return them to the hot pot. Mash with a little stock and the cream, then add salt, pepper, and nutmeg to taste. ■ Serve the meat loaves with gravy on top and with sweet potatoes and peas and radishes alongside.

chicken & guacamole
sammies

Heat a griddle pan or cast-iron skillet over medium-high heat. ■ Season the chicken with salt and pepper. Combine the remaining spices in a small bowl and rub all over the chicken. Brush the griddle or skillet with a tablespoon of EVOO. Cook the chicken for 11 to 12 minutes, turning once. Remove from the pan and let cool enough to handle; slice each piece on an angle into 4 pieces. ■ Halve, pit, and peel the avocados and dress with lime or lemon juice. Cut each half into 4 slices. ■ In a small skillet, heat the remaining tablespoon of EVOO. Add the onions, jalapeños, and garlic and sauté for a few minutes to soften. Add the tomatoes and season with salt and pepper. Turn off the heat and mix in the cilantro. ■ Place the lettuce on the roll bottoms and top each with sliced chicken and avocado, alternating the slices. Spoon on some warm salsa and cover with a roll top. Serve with a few chips alongside.

SERVES 4

4 boneless skinless **chicken breast** halves, 6 ounces each

Salt and **pepper**

1 tablespoon **sweet smoked paprika**, a palmful

½ tablespoon ground **cumin**

½ tablespoon ground **coriander**

2 tablespoons **EVOO** (extra-virgin olive oil)

2 ripe **Hass avocados**

Juice of 1 **lime** or lemon

1 small **red onion**, chopped

2 **jalapeño peppers**, seeded and thinly sliced

1 large **garlic clove**, finely chopped

1 (15-ounce) can diced **fire-roasted tomatoes**, drained

2 tablespoons fresh **cilantro** leaves, finely chopped

4 **red leaf lettuce** leaves

4 crusty, cornmeal-topped **kaiser rolls**, split

Flavored specialty corn or blue **corn chips**

chicken & broccolini
with orange sauce

SERVES 4

2¼ cups **chicken stock**, divided

1 cup **Texmati rice** or white rice

1 small bunch of **scallions**, thinly sliced on an angle

1½ pounds boneless skinless **chicken**, white or dark meat (3 breast halves or 5 to 6 thighs)

Salt and **pepper**

1 large bundle of **broccolini**, trimmed and cut into 2-inch pieces

3 tablespoons high-temperature cooking **oil**, such as canola, safflower, or peanut, divided

1 inch of fresh **gingerroot**, peeled and grated or finely chopped

3 to 4 **garlic cloves**, finely chopped

⅓ cup **tamari** (aged soy sauce), soy sauce, or low-sodium soy sauce

½ cup **orange marmalade**

Bring 1¾ cups of the stock to a boil in a medium saucepan. Stir in the rice, cover, reduce the heat to a simmer, and cook for 15 to 18 minutes, until tender. Add the scallions and fluff with a fork. ■ Bring a few inches of water to a boil for the broccolini. ■ Meanwhile, thinly slice the thighs or, if using breast meat, butterfly each breast into cutlets, then thinly slice. Season the sliced chicken with salt and pepper. ■ To the boiling water add some salt and the broccolini. Parboil the broccolini for 3 to 4 minutes, then drain, run under cool water, and reserve. ■ Heat 2 tablespoons of the oil in a large nonstick skillet over high heat. To the very hot pan, add the chicken and stir-fry until golden, no more than 5 minutes. Remove the chicken to a plate and reserve. Add the remaining tablespoon of oil to the pan, along with the ginger and garlic. Stir for 30 seconds, then add the tamari, marmalade, and the remaining ½ cup stock. Add the chicken and broccolini back to the pan to heat while the sauce is thickening. ■ Serve the chicken and broccolini over rice.

open-face turkey burgers
with potpie gravy

Combine the turkey with the fresh herbs, mustard, and salt and pepper and form 4 large patties. ■ Heat a nonstick skillet with the EVOO over medium-high heat and cook the burgers for 12 to 14 minutes, turning once, until firm and cooked through. ■ Meanwhile, for the potpie gravy, heat a small sauce pot over medium heat with the butter. When the butter melts, add the shallots, carrots, celery, and salt and pepper. Sauté for 7 to 8 minutes, then sprinkle with the flour. Stir for 1 minute, then whisk in the stock. Cook to thicken for 3 to 4 minutes, then stir in the peas and heat through. ■ Toast the English muffins. Top each half muffin with a burger and potpie gravy and serve.

SERVES 4

2 pounds **ground turkey breast**

¼ cup chopped fresh **chives**

¼ cup chopped fresh **dill**

¼ cup chopped fresh **flat-leaf parsley** leaves

2 tablespoons **Dijon mustard**

Salt and **pepper**

2 tablespoons **EVOO** (extra-virgin olive oil)

3 tablespoons **butter**

2 large **shallots**, chopped

2 **carrots**, finely chopped

2 **celery stalks**, finely chopped

2 tablespoons all-purpose **flour**

2 cups **chicken stock**

½ cup frozen **green peas**

2 sandwich-size **English muffins**

egg foo young

¼ cup **vegetable oil**

8 **eggs**

¼ pound thinly sliced **ham**, finely chopped (or chopped cooked beef, pork, chicken, shrimp, or tofu)

1 cup fresh **bean sprouts**, a few healthy handfuls

½ cup **shredded carrots**

¼ pound **shiitake mushrooms**, stemmed and thinly sliced

1 cup shredded **baby bok choy**

1 (8-ounce) can **water chestnuts**, drained and finely chopped

¼ **red bell pepper**, seeded and very thinly sliced

1 bunch of **scallions**, whites and greens, thinly sliced on an angle

1 inch of fresh **gingerroot**, peeled and grated, plus 2 thin slices

1 large **garlic clove**, grated or mashed to a paste

Salt and **pepper**

1 tablespoon **cornstarch**

1 cup **chicken stock**

¼ cup **tamari** (aged soy sauce)

1 teaspoon **hot sauce**

Heat a griddle pan over medium heat and brush it with some oil. ■ In a large mixing bowl, whisk the eggs, then stir in the ham (or substitute), bean sprouts, carrots, mushrooms, bok choy, water chestnuts, bell pepper, scallions, grated ginger, and garlic. Season with salt and pepper and mix until completely combined. Using a large spoon, drop about ½ cup of the mixture onto the heated and oiled griddle. Cook like pancakes, 2 to 3 minutes per side, until golden. ■ Meanwhile, combine the cornstarch in a small bowl with a splash of chicken stock to dissolve. Place the remaining stock, the tamari, cornstarch mixture, hot sauce, and sliced ginger in a small pot over medium heat. Cook for 3 minutes or so, until it thickens enough to coat the back of a spoon. Remove the sliced ginger and turn off the heat. ■ For each person, serve 2 Egg Foo Young cakes with gravy poured over the top.

palomilla steaks

Palomilla is the most well known steak served in Cuban restaurants. It has delicious flavors such as lime juice, onions, and garlic. *Muy delicioso!* Serve with black beans and rice alongside.

In a shallow dish, combine the vinegar, 4 tablespoons of the of EVOO, the garlic, marjoram or oregano, cilantro, and cumin. ■ Pat the steaks dry, season with salt and pepper, and give them a turn in the marinade. Let them marinate, covered, for 4 hours in the fridge. ■ Heat a skillet over medium heat with the remaining 2 tablespoons of EVOO. Add the onions, season with salt and pepper, and cook until very tender, about 20 minutes, adding the beer or stock for the last five minutes of cooking. As the onions cook, take the meat out of the fridge to bring it back up to room temperature before cooking. ■ When the onions are just about tender, heat a cast-iron skillet over medium-high to high heat. Shake the excess marinade off the steaks and cook the steaks in batches in the hot skillet until the outsides are crispy, 2 minutes on each side. Keep the finished steaks on a warm platter while you finish the rest of the steaks. When all the steaks are cooked, turn off the heat, add the butter to the pan, and when it melts, stir in the parsley and lime juice. ■ Serve the steaks immediately topped with the onions and the lime butter.

SERVES 4

2 tablespoons **vinegar**

6 tablespoons **EVOO** (extra-virgin olive oil), divided

2 **garlic cloves**, minced

1 teaspoon dried **marjoram** or oregano

2 tablespoons finely chopped fresh **cilantro** leaves

1 teaspoon ground **cumin**

4 (8- to 10-ounce) **top sirloin steaks**, very thinly sliced (if you can't get them ¼ inch thick or thinner, pound them out a bit with a mallet)

Salt and **pepper**

2 **onions**, very thinly sliced

½ cup **beer** or chicken stock

4 tablespoons (½ stick) **butter**

¼ cup fresh **flat-leaf parsley** leaves, finely chopped

Juice of 2 **limes**

meatless shepherd's pie with horseradish-cheddar potatoes

SERVES 4 TO 6

4 medium to large starchy **Idaho potatoes**, peeled and cut into chunks

2 **parsnips**, peeled and cut into thick slices

Salt

3 tablespoons **prepared horseradish**

½ cup **cream**

Black pepper

3 to 4 tablespoons chopped fresh **chives**

1½ cups **super-sharp white cheddar cheese**

1 **egg**, lightly beaten

¼ cup **EVOO** (extra-virgin olive oil)

6 medium **portabella mushroom caps**, wiped clean, gills scraped, chopped into bite-size pieces

2 sprigs of fresh **rosemary**, leaves removed and finely chopped

1 large **carrot**, peeled and chopped

1 medium-large **onion**, chopped

4 **garlic cloves**, chopped

1 small bundle of Dinosaur or Tuscan or black **kale**, stemmed and thinly sliced

Freshly grated **nutmeg**

¼ cup **Worcestershire sauce**

2½ cups **mushroom stock**, available on the soup aisle of the market, or vegetable stock

3 tablespoons **butter**

2 tablespoons all-purpose **flour**

Preheat the broiler and place a rack in the middle of the oven. Arrange individual casseroles or a large casserole on a rimmed baking sheet set near the stove. ■ Place the potatoes and parsnips in a medium pot and cover with water. Bring to a boil, salt the water, and cook until tender, 15 minutes or so. Drain and return to the hot pot. Add the horseradish, cream, salt and pepper, and chives and mash to the desired consistency. Stir in 1 cup of the cheese and the egg. ■ Meanwhile, heat a Dutch oven or large skillet over high heat with the EVOO. Add the mushrooms and rosemary and cook for 10 minutes. Then add the carrot and onions. Season liberally with salt and pepper and cook for 5 minutes more. Add the garlic and stir, then add the kale, season with nutmeg, and wilt the kale into the pan, about 2 minutes. Add the Worcestershire and stock and bring to a boil. In a small skillet, melt the butter and whisk in the flour for 1 minute, then stir into the mushroom and kale mixture to thicken. Transfer the filling to the individual casseroles or large casserole. Top the filling with the mashed potatoes, sprinkle with the remaining ½ cup of cheese, and brown under the broiler for 2 to 3 minutes.

salmon & sweet potato cakes with agrodolce relish & arugula

Place the potato in a small pot, cover with water, and bring to a boil. Salt the water and cook the potato until tender, 10 to 12 minutes. Drain, return to the pot, and mash. ■ Meanwhile, place the fillets in a skillet with the wine, bay leaf, and enough water to come up to the top of the fillets. Do not cover, bring to a boil, and reduce the heat to a simmer and poach for 8 to 10 minutes, until the fish is opaque. Remove the skin and transfer the salmon to a bowl. Flake the fish and season with salt and pepper. Add the mashed sweet potatoes to the bowl along with the Old Bay seasoning, half the cracker crumbs, the egg, thyme, hot sauce, scallions, and dill. Mix to combine. The fish cake mixture needs to be just firm enough to mold cakes. If it's too wet, add a few more cracker crumbs. ■ Heat two skillets side by side, one with 2 tablespoons of the EVOO over medium heat and the other with 1 tablespoon of EVOO over medium-high heat. Form four 4-inch patties and turn the salmon cakes in the remaining cracker crumbs, then add them to the first pan. Cook the fish cakes for 2 to 3 minutes on each side to light golden. Add the red onions, celery, and garlic to the second pan and cook for 3 to 4 minutes. Then add the tomatoes, season with salt and pepper, and cook for 2 minutes more. Stir the vinegar into the relish, then sprinkle the sugar over top and stir again. ■ Serve the fish cakes alongside the arugula with the agrodolce relish on top.

SERVES 4

1 large **sweet potato**, peeled and cut into small chunks

Salt

3 (6-ounce) **salmon fillets**, skin on

1 cup **white wine**

1 **bay leaf**

Black pepper

1 tablespoon **Old Bay seafood seasoning**, a palmful

1½ cups **saltine cracker crumbs**

1 **egg**, lightly beaten

1 tablespoon fresh **thyme leaves**, finely chopped

1 tablespoon **hot sauce**

2 **scallions**, finely chopped

3 to 4 tablespoons finely chopped fresh **dill**

3 tablespoons **EVOO** (extra-virgin olive oil)

1 small **red onion**, thinly sliced

2 small **celery stalks**, finely chopped

2 **garlic cloves**, chopped

1 pint grape or cherry **tomatoes**, halved or quartered

2 tablespoons **red wine vinegar**

1 rounded teaspoon **sugar**

4 cups **arugula** or baby arugula leaves

coconut
fish fry

4 (8-ounce) **tilapia fillets**

Salt and **pepper**

½ cup all-purpose **flour**

2 **eggs**, beaten

1 cup **panko bread crumbs**

1 cup **unsweetened grated coconut**

4 tablespoons **vegetable oil**

½ cup **pineapple preserves**

2 tablespoons **rice wine vinegar** or tamari (aged soy sauce)

¼ cup **chicken stock**

2 **scallions**, whites and greens, very thinly sliced

Serve with a **green salad** or with a slaw salad dressed with oil and vinegar.

Preheat the oven to 275°F. ■ Place a rack over a rimmed baking sheet and place in the oven. ■ Arrange 3 shallow dishes on the countertop near the stove. Season the fish with salt and pepper. Place the flour in the first dish, the eggs in the second, and the panko with the coconut in the third dish. ■ Heat a thin layer of vegetable oil, a couple tablespoons, in a large skillet over medium-high heat. Coat 2 pieces of fish in the flour, then egg, then bread crumbs, and fry until brown and crispy, 3 to 4 minutes on each side. Transfer the fish to the oven to keep warm, and repeat with the remaining 2 pieces of fish. ■ While the fish cooks, in a small pot combine the preserves, rice wine vinegar or tamari, and chicken stock. Heat through over medium heat, then stir in the scallions. Drizzle the pineapple sauce over the fish.

4

30-minute
meals

5

**yes!
the kids**
will eat it

6

sides &
starters

These recipes coordinate back to our Look +
Cook 100 meals, but feel free to mix and match
them with your favorite entrées, too. Flag your
favs as you cook your way through this section
and develop your own go-to list of starters and
sidekicks.

7

simple sauces
& bottom-of-
the-jar tips

8

desserts

spinach salad
on garlic croutons

SERVES 4 TO 6

2 large **eggs**

12 slices **crusty peasant bread**

2 large **garlic cloves**, halved

EVOO (extra-virgin olive oil) for liberal drizzling, plus 2 tablespoons

½ cup grated **Parmigiano-Reggiano** cheese

¼ pound thick-cut **pancetta**, diced

½ pound **cremini mushrooms**, sliced ¼ inch thick or quartered

Salt and **pepper**

⅓ cup **Marsala** or dry sherry

½ pound farm **spinach** (available in bundles rather than bags in produce section), washed, dried, and chopped

½ small **red onion**, chopped

Juice of 1 **lemon**

Freshly grated **nutmeg**

Preheat the oven to 400°F. ■ Place the eggs in a small pan, cover with water, and bring to a boil. Cover the pan, turn off the heat, and let stand for 10 minutes. Run the eggs under cold water, crack them, and return them to the cold water for a few minutes to loosen the shells, then peel and chop the eggs. ■ While the eggs come to a boil, arrange the bread on a baking sheet and toast in the oven for 8 to 10 minutes until golden. Remove from the oven and rub the toast with cut garlic, drizzle with EVOO, and sprinkle with the cheese. Return to the oven for 1 to 2 minutes to set the cheese into the toast. ■ While the bread toasts, heat a skillet over medium-high heat with the 2 tablespoons of EVOO. Add the pancetta to the hot oil, crisp for 3 minutes or so, then add the mushrooms and cook for 8 to 10 minutes, until tender. Season with salt and pepper and deglaze the pan with the Marsala or sherry. ■ While the mushrooms cook, combine the spinach with red onions and dress with the lemon juice, a liberal drizzle of EVOO, salt, pepper, and nutmeg. ■ To serve, arrange the toasts on a platter and top with the mushrooms, then the spinach, and garnish with the chopped eggs.

bruschetta with hot cherry tomatoes

SERVES 4 TO 6

3 tablespoons **EVOO** (extra-virgin olive oil)

3 to 4 **garlic cloves**, chopped

2 pints **cherry tomatoes**

Salt

1 teaspoon **crushed red pepper flakes**

A handful of fresh **flat-leaf parsley** leaves, chopped

Loaf of **semolina bread**, sliced

A few leaves of **basil**, torn

Heat about 2 tablespoons of the EVOO in a medium skillet over medium heat. Add the garlic, toss for 2 minutes, then add the tomatoes and season with salt and the red pepper flakes. Toss to coat the tomatoes in EVOO, cover the pan, raise the heat a bit, and cook for 10 to 12 minutes until the tomatoes burst. Meanwhile, preheat the broiler. Remove the lid, squish any late poppers with a wooden spoon, and cook the tomatoes for another minute to thicken. Stir in the parsley and adjust the seasoning, then remove from the heat. ■ Under the broiler, char the bread on both sides. Arrange the bread on a platter and top with the hot tomatoes, garnish with torn basil, drizzle with the remaining tablespoon of EVOO, and serve.

milanese fettuccine alfredo

SERVES 6 (unless I'm one of them . . . then it serves 1)

½ teaspoon **saffron threads**, 2 pinches

1 cup **chicken stock**

Salt

1 pound **fettuccine**

6 tablespoons (¾ stick) **butter**, cut into pats

8 ounces (2½ to 3 cups loosely packed) finely grated **Parmigiano-Reggiano** cheese

Bring a large pot of water to a boil. ■ Preheat the oven to warm. Place a large serving bowl or platter for pasta in the oven to warm. ■ In a small pot over low heat, steep the saffron threads in the stock. ■ When the water boils, season with salt, add the pasta, and cook to al dente. Just before draining, place a ladle of starchy water in the pot with the saffron stock. Drain the pasta. ■ Scatter the butter pats over the warm bowl or platter, then place the pasta over top. Pour the saffron liquid over the pasta and scatter in half of the cheese, toss for 1 minute, add more cheese, and continue to toss for another 1 to 2 minutes, until the pasta is evenly coated and the cheese has melted into the saffron broth to form a creamy, lightly golden sauce. Serve immediately.

spinach salad with slumped mushrooms

SERVES 4

8 very large **white mushroom caps**, very thinly sliced

1 small **red onion**, very thinly sliced

2 teaspoons grated **lemon zest**

Juice of 2 **lemons**

⅓ cup **EVOO** (extra-virgin olive oil)

Salt and **pepper**

1 teaspoon **ground fennel** or a sprinkle of fennel seed

½ teaspoon **crushed red pepper flakes**

3 bundles of farm **spinach** (available in bundles rather than bags in produce section), trimmed and washed

Combine the mushroom caps and onions in a bowl and dress with the lemon zest and juice and EVOO, then season with salt and pepper, the ground fennel, and the red pepper flakes. Let stand for 20 minutes or until softened and slumped. Chop the spinach and arrange in a large shallow bowl. Top with the mushrooms and onions and gently toss to wilt the spinach.

sweet onion potatoes au gratin

SERVES 4

2 tablespoons **butter**

1 large or 2 medium **sweet onions**, such as Vidalia, thinly sliced

Salt and **pepper**

½ teaspoon ground **thyme**, or dried if ground isn't available

1 **bay leaf**, fresh or dried

2 pounds baby **Yukon Gold potatoes** or fingerling potatoes

½ to ⅔ cup **cream**

½ cup grated **Parmigiano-Reggiano** cheese

½ pound grated **Gruyère** or other Swiss cheese

Heat a skillet with the butter over medium heat. Add the onions, season with salt, pepper, the thyme, and the bay leaf, and cook until very soft and sweet and lightly caramelized, about 20 minutes. Remove the bay leaf. ■ While the onions cook, place the potatoes in a pot and cover with water. Bring to a boil, salt the water, and cook until tender, 12 to 15 minutes. Drain and return to the hot pot. Mash the potatoes with the cream, season with salt and pepper, and mash in the Parm cheese. ■ Preheat the broiler. Arrange the mashed potatoes in individual gratin dishes or a shallow casserole. Top the potatoes with the onions and Gruyère cheese. Brown the gratins under the hot broiler until bubbly, about 2 minutes.

spinach, mushroom & balsamic-cream crostini

SERVES 4 to 6

12 slices **peasant bread**

1 pound **cremini mushrooms**, wiped clean

3 tablespoons **EVOO** (extra-virgin olive oil)

3 to 4 **garlic cloves**, grated or finely chopped

Salt and **pepper**

3 to 4 handfuls of fresh **baby spinach**

Freshly grated **nutmeg**

¼ cup aged **balsamic vinegar**

¼ cup **heavy cream**

Preheat the oven to 375°F. Toast the bread on a rack over a rimmed baking sheet for 10 minutes or until lightly golden. ■ Quarter the mushrooms. In a large skillet, heat the EVOO over medium-high heat. Add the mushrooms and cook until deeply golden and tender, about 10 minutes. ■ Once the mushrooms have started to brown up, add the garlic and season with salt and pepper. Chop the spinach coarsely, then stir in to wilt. Season with a few grates of nutmeg, stir in the vinegar for 1 minute, then add the cream, heat for a minute more, and remove from the heat. Transfer the spinach and mushrooms to a small bowl and serve as a topping for the toasted bread.

spinach fettuccine with gorgonzola cream & spinach

SERVES 4

Salt

1½ (12-ounce) packages **spinach fettuccine**, 18 ounces total

2 tablespoons **butter**

2 **garlic cloves**, finely chopped

2 tablespoons all-purpose **flour**

1 cup **chicken stock**

1 cup **cream**

8 ounces **Gorgonzola cheese**, cut into small pieces

A few leaves of **fresh sage**, finely chopped

Freshly ground **black pepper**

4 handfuls of **baby spinach leaves**

Bring a large pot of water to a boil for the pasta, salt the water, and cook the pasta to al dente. ■ Heat the butter in a large sauce pot. Add the garlic, cook for 2 minutes, then whisk in the flour and cook for 1 minute. Whisk in the stock, then the cream; bring to a bubble and stir in the Gorgonzola. Cook, stirring, for about 2 minutes, until the Gorgonzola is melted. Stir in the sage and a little pepper and cook for 3 minutes more. ■ In a serving bowl, toss the hot pasta with the sauce and fresh spinach to wilt in.

chunky puttanesca crostini

1 loaf **crusty bread**, thinly sliced

¼ cup **EVOO** (extra-virgin olive oil)

6 to 8 large **Italian anchovy fillets**

4 **garlic cloves**, chopped

1 teaspoon **crushed red pepper flakes**

2 pints **grape tomatoes**

4 tablespoons **capers**, drained

¼ cup chopped pitted **oil-cured olives**

½ cup fresh **flat-leaf parsley** leaves, chopped

Preheat the oven to 325°F. Arrange the bread on rimmed baking sheets in a single layer and toast until evenly golden, about 12 minutes. ■ Heat the EVOO in a skillet with a tight-fitting lid over medium to medium-high heat. Melt the anchovies into the oil. When they break up and melt away, stir in the garlic, red pepper flakes, tomatoes, capers, and olives and cover the pan. Cook for 7 to 8 minutes more to burst the tomatoes, then uncover and mash any stray tomatoes with a potato masher or wooden spoon, and fold in the parsley. ■ Spoon the chunky sauce onto the crostini and serve immediately.

corny polenta

1 tablespoon **EVOO** (extra-virgin olive oil)

2 ears **fresh husked corn** on the cob or 1 cup defrosted kernels

3 to 4 thin **scallions**, finely chopped

3 cups **chicken stock**

1 cup **quick-cooking polenta**

2 tablespoons **butter**

2 tablespoons **hot sauce**, or to taste

Salt

Heat the EVOO in a sauce pot over medium-high heat. Balance each corn cob on a small inverted bowl nested in a larger bowl. Cut the kernels off the cob from top to bottom with a sharp knife. ■ Sauté the corn in the hot oil until it starts to brown at the edges, 3 to 4 minutes. Add the scallions and cook for a minute, then add the stock and bring to a boil. Whisk in the polenta and cook to thicken for 2 to 3 minutes, then melt in the butter and season with hot sauce and salt to taste.

red white beans

SERVES 4 to 6

Heat the EVOO in a large skillet over medium heat, add the onions, and season with rosemary, salt, and pepper. Cook the onions until soft, 8 to 10 minutes. Stir in the tomato paste for 1 minute, stir in the stock, then stir in the beans and reduce the heat to low. Adjust the seasoning and keep warm until ready to serve.

2 tablespoons **EVOO** (extra-virgin olive oil)

1 medium-large **onion**, chopped

2 sprigs of fresh **rosemary**, leaves removed and finely chopped

Salt and **pepper**

¼ cup **tomato paste**

1 cup **chicken stock**

2 (15-ounce) cans **cannellini beans**, drained

lentil-potato salad

SERVES 4 TO 6

Serve this salad with Almost Tandoori Chicken (page 153) or with Crispy Curry Fried Chicken (page 151).

Place the onion halves, bay leaf, and lentils in a medium pot, cover with water, and bring to a boil. Simmer for 10 minutes, add the potatoes, and cook for 7 to 8 minutes more. ■ While the lentils and potatoes cook, heat a tablespoon of the EVOO in a medium skillet and sauté the shallots, garlic, and bell pepper for a couple minutes. Then add the peas and heat through for a minute more. Transfer to a shallow bowl to cool. ■ In a food processor, process the stock, mint, and cilantro into a paste and add to the bowl. ■ Drain the lentils and potatoes, discard the onions and bay leaf, and return the lentils and potatoes to the hot pot to dry for a minute. Then add to the bowl with the herb paste and vegetables. Add the remaining 3 tablespoons of EVOO to the salad and toss. Season with the cumin and with salt and pepper to taste.

1 small **onion**, halved

1 fresh **bay leaf**

1 cup **lentils**

1 large **Idaho potato**, peeled and cut into small dice

4 tablespoons **EVOO** (extra-virgin olive oil)

1 large **shallot**, chopped

2 **garlic cloves**, chopped

½ **red bell pepper**, seeded and chopped

½ cup **frozen peas**

⅓ cup **vegetable stock**

½ cup packed fresh **mint leaves**

½ cup packed fresh **cilantro** or baby spinach leaves

½ teaspoon ground **cumin**

Salt and **pepper**

pine nut–saffron pilaf

1 tablespoon **EVOO** (extra-virgin olive oil)

¼ cup **pine nuts**

2 tablespoons **butter**

A handful of **thin spaghetti**, broken into small pieces

¼ teaspoon **saffron threads**

1 cup **rice**

2 cups **chicken stock**

A handful of **golden raisins** or sultanas

Heat the EVOO in a sauce pot over medium heat. Add the nuts and toast until lightly golden, then remove and reserve. ■ Melt the butter in the pot, then add the broken pasta and toast to golden. Stir in the saffron and rice, then add the stock. Bring to a boil, stir in the raisins, then cover and simmer for 17 to 18 minutes, until the liquid has been absorbed and the pasta and rice are tender. ■ Fluff the pilaf with a fork and stir in the reserved nuts. Serve immediately.

brown rice with orange

1¾ cups **chicken stock**

1 cup **brown rice**

1 tablespoon **butter**

Salt and **pepper**

1 **orange**

¼ cup fresh **cilantro** leaves, finely chopped

4 **scallions**, whites and greens, finely chopped

In a medium pot over medium-high heat, combine the chicken stock, rice, butter, salt and pepper, and 1 teaspoon orange zest. Bring the liquid up to a bubble, then cover the pot. Reduce the heat to medium-low and simmer until all of the liquid has been absorbed, about 40 minutes. When the rice is cooked, fluff with a fork and stir in the juice of the orange, the cilantro, and the scallions.

greek salad with yogurt dressing

In a large salad bowl, whisk together the lemon juice, yogurt, garlic, EVOO, and salt and pepper to taste. ■ Add the cucumber, tomatoes, bell pepper, parsley, and onions and toss to coat with the dressing. Garnish with the olives and hot peppers.

SERVES 4

Juice of 1 **lemon**

½ cup **Greek yogurt**

1 small **garlic clove**, finely chopped and mashed into a paste or grated

¼ cup **EVOO** (extra-virgin olive oil)

Salt and **pepper**

½ **seedless cucumber**, diced

2 **tomatoes**, seeded and diced

1 **bell pepper**, seeded and diced

1 cup fresh **flat-leaf parsley** leaves, chopped

½ **red onion**, diced

½ cup pitted **kalamata olives**

4 to 5 **Greek hot peppers**, chopped

chorizo mushroom queso dip

Heat the EVOO in a small skillet over medium-high heat. Dice and brown the Spanish chorizo to render the fat, or remove the casing of fresh Mexican chorizo, then brown and crumble. Preheat the broiler. Add the mushroom caps to the skillet and cook with the sausage until just tender, 6 to 7 minutes. Transfer to a small casserole or baking dish, top with the cheese, and place under the broiler until bubbly, 1 to 2 minutes. Top with the scallions and serve with chips for dipping.

SERVES 4 to 6

½ tablespoon **EVOO** (extra-virgin olive oil), a drizzle

½ pound Spanish or Mexican **chorizo**

½ pound **mushroom caps**, quartered

1 cup diced **Mexican melting cheese** or Monterey Jack or pepper Jack cheese

2 **scallions**, thinly sliced

1 bag **corn tortilla chips** or blue corn tortilla chips, any variety

fennel & pepper salad

SERVES 4

1 large or 2 small to medium **fresh fennel bulbs**

2 **large bell peppers**, 1 red and 1 yellow, seeded and very thinly sliced

1 head of **radicchio**, halved and shredded

Juice of 1 **lemon**

2 tablespoons **EVOO** (extra-virgin olive oil), eyeball it

Salt and **pepper**

Chop and reserve ¼ cup of the fennel fronds. Then trim the bulbs, halve them, and very thinly slice by hand or with a mandoline, and pile into a bowl. Add the bell peppers, radicchio, lemon juice, a healthy douse of **EVOO**, the fennel fronds, and salt and pepper. Toss, let stand for 15 minutes, toss again, and serve.

garlicky creamed corn & spinach

SERVES 4 to 6

2 tablespoons **butter**

Fresh **corn kernels**, scraped from 6 ears of corn or 3 cups frozen corn kernels

2 large **garlic cloves**, finely chopped

Salt and **pepper**

½ cup **heavy cream**

Freshly grated **nutmeg**

2 bundles of farm **spinach** (available in bundles rather than bags in produce section), about ½ pound trimmed weight, chopped

Heat a large skillet over medium heat with the butter, add the corn and starchy liquid from the scraped cobs, and cook for 5 minutes. Stir in the garlic, season with salt and pepper, and cook for 2 to 3 minutes more. Add the cream and nutmeg to taste and cook, stirring occasionally, over medium-low heat for about 15 minutes, until very creamy. Wilt in the spinach, adjust the seasonings, and serve.

pimiento rice

SERVES 4

2 tablespoons **EVOO** (extra-virgin olive oil)

2 **garlic cloves**, finely chopped or grated

1½ cups **long-grain white rice**

2½ cups **chicken stock**

Salt and **pepper**

2 (4-ounce) jars **chopped pimientos**

½ **red onion**, finely chopped

Place a medium pot over medium-high heat with the EVOO. Add the garlic and cook for about 1 minute. Add the rice and toss to coat in the garlic oil. Add the chicken stock, season with salt and pepper, and bring the liquid up to a bubble. Reduce the heat to low, cover the pot, and cook until all of the liquid has been absorbed, about 15 minutes. ■ When the rice is ready, fluff with a fork and stir in the pimientos and red onions. Serve warm or at room temperature.

green beans
with crispy bacon

SERVES 6

2 pounds **green beans**, trimmed

A drizzle of **EVOO** (extra-virgin olive oil)

6 slices **bacon**, chopped

1 teaspoon **coarse black pepper**

¼ cup cider or red wine **vinegar**

2 teaspoons **sugar**

In a large skillet, bring a couple of inches of water to a boil. Cook the green beans in the boiling water until al dente, about 3 to 5 minutes, then drain. In the same skillet, heat a drizzle of oil over medium-high heat. When hot, add the bacon and pepper and cook until the bacon is crisp, about 5 minutes, then drain off all but 2 tablespoons or so of the fat. Toss the beans in the fat with the bacon and season with the vinegar and sugar.

pico de gallo pilaf

1 tablespoon **EVOO** (extra-virgin olive oil)

½ cup **orzo pasta**

1 cup **white rice**

2 cups **chicken** or **vegetable stock**

4 **plum tomatoes**, seeded and finely chopped

1 small **onion**, red or white, finely chopped

1 **jalapeño pepper**, seeded and finely chopped

A handful of fresh **cilantro leaves**, finely chopped

Zest and juice of 1 **lime**

Salt

Heat the EVOO in a sauce pot over medium heat, add the orzo, and toast to a deep golden color. Add the rice and stir gently to combine with the toasted pasta. Add the stock and bring to a boil, then cover the pot and simmer for 17 to 18 minutes, until the orzo and rice are tender. ■ In a small bowl, combine the tomatoes, onions, jalapeño, cilantro, and lime zest and juice, and season with salt to taste. ■ When the orzo and rice are cooked, fluff with a fork and combine with the salsa.

tangy goat cheese
& dill potato salad

2½ pounds diced **Yukon Gold potatoes**

Salt

¼ cup **white wine** or 2 tablespoons white wine vinegar

½ cup **goat cheese crumbles**

1 cup **yogurt**, crème fraîche, or sour cream

Juice of 1 **lemon**

¼ cup **EVOO** (extra-virgin olive oil)

1 small **garlic clove**, finely grated or mashed to a paste

¼ cup finely chopped fresh **dill**

4 **scallions**, whites and greens, finely chopped

Black pepper

2 **dill pickles**, chopped

4 **radishes**, thinly sliced

In a large pot, cover the potatoes with water and bring to a boil, then salt the water and cook until tender, about 10 minutes. ■ When the potatoes are cooked, return them to the hot pot and douse with the wine or white wine vinegar. ■ In a large bowl, whisk together the goat cheese, yogurt, lemon juice, EVOO, and garlic. Toss the potatoes, dill, and scallions in the dressing and season with salt and pepper. Garnish with chopped pickles and thinly sliced radishes and serve.

tabbouleh salad
with nuts

SERVES 6

Bring 1 cup water to a boil. Place the bulgur wheat into a heat-proof bowl, pour the boiling water over the bulgur, and let stand for 15 minutes. ■ Place the nuts in a small dry skillet and lightly toast, then remove and cool the nuts. ■ In a salad bowl, combine the cumin with the lemon zest and juice and whisk in the EVOO. Add the bulgur, mint, parsley, scallions, tomatoes, cucumber, and salt to taste, toss, and let stand for a few minutes. Adjust the seasoning and toss again. Serve.

¾ cup **bulgur wheat**

2 handfuls of **pine nuts** or slivered almonds

1 teaspoon ground **cumin**

Zest and juice of 1 **lemon**

¼ cup **EVOO** (extra-virgin olive oil)

¼ cup fresh **mint leaves**, chopped

½ cup fresh **flat-leaf parsley** leaves, chopped

4 **scallions**, whites and greens, chopped

2 **plum tomatoes**, seeded and chopped

½ **seedless cucumber**, peeled and chopped

Salt

stuffed baby bellas

16 **baby portabella mushrooms** (creminis)

1 pound **ground chicken** or turkey breast

1 teaspoon **fennel seed**, ⅓ palmful

1 small **onion**, finely chopped

3 **garlic cloves**, grated or finely chopped

1 **lemon**

1 cup **shredded asiago cheese**

½ cup **bread crumbs**, a couple handfuls

1 (10-ounce) box **frozen chopped spinach**, defrosted and wrung dry in a clean kitchen towel

Salt and **pepper**

2 tablespoons **EVOO** (extra-virgin olive oil)

¼ cup **pine nuts** or chopped almonds

Wipe the mushrooms clean with a damp cloth. Remove the stems and finely chop them. ■ Preheat the oven to 400°F. ■ In a large mixing bowl, combine the ground meat, fennel seed, onions, garlic, lemon zest, half of the cheese, the chopped mushroom stems, bread crumbs, and spinach, and season with salt and pepper. Season the mushroom caps as well with salt and pepper. Brush lightly with EVOO and stuff the mixture into the caps. ■ Arrange the caps on a rimmed baking sheet or in a baking dish. Leave some room around each mushroom to prevent the caps from getting steamy. Sprinkle the remaining cheese and the nuts on the caps and transfer to the oven. Bake until the mushrooms are tender and the filling is cooked through, about 25 minutes. ■ Serve warm.

blt mac 'n' cheese stuffed tomatoes

Salt

¼ pound **elbow macaroni**

4 slices **bacon**, chopped

2 **leeks**, halved lengthwise, thinly sliced crosswise, washed, and dried

2 tablespoons all-purpose **flour**

1 cup **chicken stock**

½ cup **whole milk**

Black pepper

2 cups grated **aged sharp cheddar cheese** (14 ounces)

8 large **Roma tomatoes**, halved lengthwise and seeded, or 8 vine-ripe tomatoes, tops cut off and scooped clean

½ cup **bread crumbs**

Preheat the oven to 400°F. ■ Bring a large pot of water to a boil over high heat. Add salt and the pasta, and cook just shy of al dente. ■ While the pasta is cooking, heat a medium-size skillet over medium heat and add the bacon. Cook until crispy, about 5 minutes, then add the leeks and cook until tender, about 2 minutes more. Add the flour and cook, stirring, for 1 minute. Whisk in the stock, milk, and salt and pepper and bring up to a bubble. Stir in 1½ cups of the cheese in a figure-eight motion. ■ Drain the pasta and combine it with the sauce. Spoon the pasta into the tomato shells and garnish with the remaining ½ cup of cheese and the bread crumbs. Place the tomato shells on a rimmed baking sheet and bake for 12 to 15 minutes, until golden brown on top.

mac 'n' cheese
jalapeño poppers

Preheat the oven to 425°F. ■ Working lengthwise, slice off the top quarter of each jalapeño. Using a small spoon or paring knife, scrape the seeds and ribs out of each jalapeño. Finely chop the tops. ■ Place a large pot of water over high heat to boil. When the water reaches a bubble, salt it well and drop in the pasta. Cook to al dente. Drain well. ■ While the pasta is cooking, place a medium pot over medium heat with the butter. Add the chopped pepper tops to the butter and cook to soften, 2 to 3 minutes. Sprinkle the flour over the peppers and cook for 1 minute more. Whisk the chicken stock and milk into the mixture and bring up to a bubble. Stir in the mustard, season the sauce with salt and black pepper, and simmer until thickened, 2 to 3 minutes. Remove the pot from the heat and stir in 1 cup of the cheese until melted. Add the pasta to the cheese sauce and stir to combine. ■ Mound up spoonfuls of the mac 'n' cheese in the peppers and place the peppers in a baking dish. Sprinkle the remaining cheese and the bread crumbs over the filling, and bake until the tops are golden brown and the peppers are tender, about 15 minutes.

SERVES 4 TO 6

16 **jalapeño peppers**

Salt

½ pound **ditalini pasta**

2 tablespoons **butter**

2 tablespoons all-purpose **flour**

½ cup **chicken stock**

1 cup **whole milk**

1 tablespoon **yellow mustard**

Black pepper

1¼ cups grated **sharp cheddar cheese**, divided

¼ cup **bread crumbs** or crushed saltine crackers

buffalo chicken
jalapeño poppers

Preheat the oven to 425°F. ■ Working lengthwise, slice off the top quarter of each jalapeño. Using a small spoon or paring knife, scrape the seeds and ribs out of each jalapeño. ■ Place a small sauce pot over low heat. Add the hot sauce and whisk in the butter until melted. Pour the sauce into a medium-size bowl and mix in the chicken, chopped celery, Monterey Jack, and half of the blue cheese. ■ Lightly mound some of the chicken mixture into each jalapeño. Place the peppers in a baking dish and top with the remaining blue cheese. ■ Bake the peppers until tender and heated through, about 15 minutes. Serve warm with carrot and celery sticks.

SERVES 4 TO 6

20 **jalapeño peppers**

⅓ cup **hot sauce**

2 tablespoons **butter**

2 cups shredded store-bought **rotisserie chicken** (skin and bones removed)

1 **celery stalk**, finely chopped

½ cup shredded **Monterey Jack** cheese

½ cup **blue cheese crumbles**

Carrot sticks, for garnish

Celery sticks, for garnish

sausage & peppers sliders

MAKES 8 SLIDERS

3 tablespoons **EVOO** (extra-virgin olive oil)

1 medium **onion**, thinly sliced

½ small **red bell pepper**, seeded and thinly sliced

½ small **green bell pepper** or 1 small cubanelle pepper, seeded and thinly sliced

2 **garlic cloves**, finely chopped or grated

1 tablespoon **Worcestershire sauce**

Salt and **pepper**

1 pound bulk sweet or hot **Italian sausage** or sausage links, casing removed

8 cubes of **Provolone cheese**, ½ inch thick and 1 inch square

8 small **dinner rolls** or packaged slider rolls, such as Pepperidge Farm brand, split open and toasted

Place a large skillet over medium-high heat with 2 tablespoons of EVOO. Add the onions, bell peppers, and garlic to the pan and cook until the veggies are tender, 7 to 8 minutes. When the veggies are tender, add the Worcestershire and season with salt and pepper. ■ While the veggies are cooking, place a second skillet over medium-high heat with the remaining tablespoon of EVOO. Shape the sausage into thin patties and wrap the meat around the cubed cheese. Cook the patties for 4 minutes on each side, or until they're deep brown and firm. ■ Place the patties on roll bottoms and top with the peppers and onions. Set the roll tops in place and serve.

twice-baked-potato fritters

Heat a large skillet over medium heat and cook the bacon until golden brown. Remove to a paper-towel-lined platter to drain. ■ In a large mixing bowl, combine the cooled mashed potatoes, sour cream, cheddar cheese, scallions, egg, cooked bacon, and salt and pepper. Mix well. ■ Pour the potato flakes into a shallow dish and place next to your bowl. ■ Drop a well-rounded tablespoonful of potato mixture into the potato flakes. Roll around in the potato flakes and form a 2-inch ball. ■ The potato fritter balls may be refrigerated, covered, for up to 2 days. ■ In a medium pot, heat a few inches of frying oil over medium-high heat. When the oil is ready, bubbles will stream rapidly away from the handle of a wooden spoon inserted in the oil. If you have a kitchen thermometer, 350°F is the ideal temperature. ■ Fry the potato balls a few at a time, making sure not to crowd the pot, 4 to 5 minutes or until golden brown. Drain on a cooling rack over a paper-towel-lined baking sheet. Repeat until all the potato balls are fried.

SERVES 6

4 slices **bacon**, chopped

1 cup **mashed potatoes**, use leftovers or make fresh from 4 medium potatoes

¼ cup **sour cream**

½ cup grated **cheddar cheese**

½ bunch of **scallions**, sliced

1 **egg**

Salt and **pepper**

1 cup **dried potato flakes**

Canola oil, for frying

chili-cheese potato
armadillos

A Tex-Mex twist on classic Hasselback potatoes!

SERVES 4

1 thick slice good-quality **white bread**, such as a pullman loaf

4 tablespoons (½ stick) **butter**

2 teaspoons **hot sauce**

1 tablespoon **chili powder**, a palmful

1½ teaspoons **sweet smoked paprika**, ½ palmful

1 teaspoon **garlic powder** or granulated garlic, ⅓ palmful

½ cup shredded **sharp yellow cheddar cheese**, a couple handfuls

¼ cup grated **Parmigiano-Reggiano** cheese, a handful

4 large **red-skin potatoes**, cleaned

EVOO (extra-virgin olive oil), for drizzling

Salt and **pepper**

Preheat the oven to 250°F. Place a rack in the middle of the oven. ■ Pulse the bread in a food processor to form soft crumbs. Scatter the crumbs on a rimmed baking sheet and toast for 15 minutes, or until light golden. Raise the oven temperature to 450°F. ■ Let the crumbs cool in a bowl and melt the butter. Toss the crumbs with the butter, hot sauce, chili powder, paprika, garlic powder, and cheeses. ■ Cover the cooled baking sheet with parchment paper. Trim a thin slice off the bottom of each potato to give it stability. Trim the ends, then thinly slice the potato across, but not all the way through; stop ¼ inch shy of all the way through. Slices should be ⅛ inch thick to no more than ¼ inch thick. ■ Gently fan out the potato slices and rinse off the starchy juice. Turn the potatoes cut side down on a microwave-safe dish and microwave on high for 10 minutes. Let cool enough to handle, about 5 minutes, then set the potatoes cut side up on the parchment-lined baking sheet, leaving lots of room around each potato. Coat with a liberal drizzle of EVOO and season with salt and pepper. ■ Roast the potatoes for 30 minutes, then remove from the oven and gently stuff the chili-cheese mixture in the ridges of the potatoes. Turn on the broiler and broil the potatoes in the middle of the oven until deeply brown and bubbly, 3 to 5 minutes.

chili meatball bites with cheesy dipper

Preheat the oven to 400°F. ■ Place a medium skillet over medium-high heat with the 2 tablespoons of EVOO. Add the onions, bell pepper, and garlic to the pan, and cook until the veggies are tender, about 5 minutes. Add the spices to the pan and cook for another minute. ■ Season the veggies with salt and pepper and transfer to a bowl to cool. Spread the crushed chips out on a plate or in a pie dish and reserve. ■ When the veggies are cool, add the beans and meat to the bowl, season with salt and pepper, and combine. Shape the mixture into two-bite-size balls and roll each of them in the crushed chips. Arrange the meatball bites on a rimmed baking sheet, drizzle lightly with EVOO, and bake until golden brown and cooked through, about 15 minutes. ■ While the meatballs are baking, place a pot over medium heat with the butter. When the butter has melted, sprinkle the flour over top and cook for about 1 minute. Whisk the stock and milk into the butter-flour mixture and bring up to a bubble. Season with salt and pepper, and simmer until thickened, about 2 minutes. Remove the pot from the heat and whisk in the cheese until melted. ■ Serve the chili meatball bites with the cheesy dipper alongside.

SERVES 6 TO 8

2 tablespoons **EVOO** (extra-virgin olive oil), plus extra for drizzling

1 small **onion**, finely chopped

1 **bell pepper**, seeded and finely chopped

2 to 3 **garlic cloves**, finely chopped or grated

2 tablespoons **chili powder**

2 teaspoons ground **cumin**

Salt and **pepper**

1½ to 2 cups **crushed tortilla chips** (just use the bits in the bottom of the bag)

1 (14.5-ounce) can **kidney beans**, drained, rinsed, and patted dry

1½ pounds **ground sirloin**

2 tablespoons **butter**

2 tablespoons all-purpose **flour**

½ cup **beef stock**

1 cup **milk**

1 cup shredded **sharp yellow cheddar cheese**

roasted pumpkin penne
with autumn pesto

SERVES 6 TO 8

1 cup fresh **flat-leaf parsley** leaves, packed

1 cup baby **spinach** or farm spinach (available in bundles rather than bags in produce section), packed

1 inch of fresh **gingerroot**, peeled and grated or minced

2 **garlic cloves**, grated or mashed into a paste with salt

½ cup chopped **walnuts**, toasted

1 teaspoon grated **lemon zest** plus juice of ½ lemon, about 2 tablespoons

Salt and **pepper**

⅓ cup plus 2 tablespoons **EVOO** (extra-virgin olive oil)

1 medium **sugar pumpkin** or butternut squash, peeled and cut into ¾-inch cubes

1 teaspoon **sweet paprika**

Freshly grated **nutmeg**

1 pound **whole-wheat penne** or semolina penne rigate (ridged penne)

½ cup grated **Parmigiano-Reggiano** cheese

Lightly salted, toasted **pumpkin seeds**, available in bulk foods section (optional)

Preheat the oven to 400°F. ■ Place the parsley, spinach, ginger, garlic, nuts, lemon zest and juice, and salt and pepper in a food processor and turn the processor on. Stream about ⅓ cup of the EVOO into the processor to form a pesto sauce. ■ Drizzle the pumpkin cubes with the 2 tablespoons of EVOO and season with salt, pepper, the paprika, and nutmeg to taste. Roast for 15 minutes, turn the cubes over, and roast for 15 minutes more. ■ Meanwhile, bring the water to a boil for the pasta, salt it, and cook the pasta to al dente, according to package directions. Reserve 1 cup of the starchy water just before draining. Drain the pasta, return it to the hot pot, add the reserved water and the pesto, and toss to coat. Gently mix in the roasted pumpkin cubes and serve topped with lots of cheese and some pumpkin seeds, if desired.

cheesy
bacon-fennel dip

Preheat the oven to 400°F. ■ In a skillet over medium heat, cook the bacon until crisp. Drain on a paper-towel-lined plate and reserve. ■ Add the fennel and garlic to the skillet with the bacon drippings and cook over medium heat for about 10 minutes, stirring occasionally, until the fennel is just tender and begins to brown. Remove from the heat. ■ Add the cream cheese, sour cream, Gorgonzola, reserved bacon, and salt and pepper to the fennel and mix well. ■ Place the mixture in individual crocks or a shallow casserole dish. ■ In a small bowl, combine the Parmigiano, bread crumbs, and parsley; top the fennel mixture with the bread-crumb mixture and bake, uncovered, for 15 minutes, until just heated through and the tops are light brown. ■ Serve with the radishes, endives, and bread as dippers alongside.

SERVES 8 TO 12

8 slices **bacon**, chopped

1 large **fennel bulb**, trimmed and chopped

2 **garlic cloves**, grated or finely chopped

1 (8-ounce) package **cream cheese**, at room temperature

⅓ to ¼ cup **sour cream**

¼ cup **crumbled domestic Gorgonzola cheese**

Salt and **pepper**

3 tablespoons grated **Parmigiano-Reggiano** cheese

3 tablespoons seasoned **bread crumbs**

¼ cup chopped fresh **flat-leaf parsley** leaves

1 bunch of **radishes**, trimmed and cleaned

2 **Belgian endives**, leaves separated and cleaned

Breads for dipping and topping, such as pumpernickel or whole-grain

bitter
caesar salad

1 rounded teaspoon **anchovy paste**

2 teaspoons **Dijon mustard**

1 **garlic clove**, grated or minced

1 teaspoon **Worcestershire sauce**

Juice of 1 **lemon**

⅓ cup **EVOO** (extra-virgin olive oil)

½ cup grated **Pecorino Romano** cheese

Coarse black pepper

2 small heads or 1 large head **escarole**, coarsely chopped or torn

1 head **treviso** (long-leaf radicchio), coarsely chopped or torn

1 cup store-bought good-quality **croutons** or 2 to 3 slices semolina bread, toasted and cubed

In a small bowl, whisk together the anchovy paste, mustard, garlic, Worcestershire, and lemon juice. Stream in the EVOO to form the dressing, then stir in the cheese and lots of black pepper. Add the greens and croutons and toss to combine.

breakfast crostini

1 pint **bocconcini** (small bites of fresh mozzarella in water)

1 (¼-inch-thick) slice **prosciutto**

1 pint multicolored baby or grape **tomatoes** or red grape tomatoes

4 thin **scallions**, whites and greens, trimmed

A handful of fresh **basil leaves**, thinly sliced

A handful of fresh **flat-leaf parsley** leaves, finely chopped

3 tablespoons **EVOO** (extra-virgin olive oil)

Salt and **pepper**

8 slices **peasant bread**

Halve the cheese bites and place in a bowl. Finely dice the prosciutto, then halve the tomatoes and add to the bowl with the cheese. Thinly slice the scallions and add the scallions and herbs to the bowl. Dress the salad with the EVOO and salt and pepper. ■ Char the bread in the oven or under the broiler. Serve with the salad for topping.

stuffed young zucchini

Preheat the oven to 425°F. ■ Halve the zucchini lengthwise and scoop out the seedy-soft center flesh with a spoon to produce a set of shallow shells to hold the stuffing. Arrange the small hulls in a baking dish. Drizzle with EVOO and season with salt and pepper. Chop up the scraped zucchini flesh and reserve. ■ Heat the remaining EVOO in a skillet over medium-high heat and sauté the mushrooms, onions, and garlic for 5 minutes. Add the zucchini flesh and tomatoes, season with salt and pepper, heat through for 1 minute, then remove from the heat. ■ While the veggies cook, toast the bread in a toaster, then butter it liberally, and tear it up, and add it to a food processor. Add the parsley and tarragon or basil and pulse into herb crumbs. ■ Fold the herb crumbs into the veggies and stir together with ½ cup of the Parm and the egg. Overstuff the zucchini shells and roast them for 15 minutes, top with remaining ¼ cup of cheese, and place under the broiler for 2 to 3 minutes more to brown.

SERVES 4

4 small **zucchini**, 5 to 6 inches long and 1½ inches thick

2 tablespoons **EVOO** (extra-virgin olive oil)

Salt and **pepper**

12 **cremini mushrooms**, chopped

1 small to medium yellow **onion**, chopped

3 to 4 **garlic cloves**, grated or chopped

2 vine-ripe **tomatoes** or Roma tomatoes, seeded and chopped

2 slices **white toasting bread**

Softened **butter**

A small handful of fresh **flat-leaf parsley** leaves

A few sprigs of fresh **tarragon** or a small handful of fresh basil leaves

¾ cup shredded **Parmigiano-Reggiano** cheese

1 **egg**, beaten

buffalo stuffed skins

4 large **Idaho potatoes**

Salt and **pepper**

3 tablespoons **EVOO** (extra-virgin olive oil), divided

1 tablespoon **butter**

1½ to 2 pounds **ground chicken breast**

1 large **carrot**, peeled and finely chopped

1 large **onion**, chopped

2 **celery stalks**, finely chopped

2 **garlic cloves**, chopped

1 tablespoon **smoked paprika** (you can substitute with chipotles or chipotle chili powder)

1 **bay leaf**

2½ cups **chicken stock**

¼ to ½ cup **hot sauce**, depending on how hot you like it

1 (15-ounce) can **tomato sauce**

¾ pound **blue cheese** (preferably Maytag), crumbled

1 **egg**

½ cup **sour cream**

6 **scallions** sliced on bias, whites and green kept separate

Preheat the oven to 350°F. ■ Place the potatoes on a rimmed baking sheet and rub them with salt, pepper, and 1 tablespoon of the EVOO. Bake for about 1 hour, until tender. ■ While the potatoes are baking, place a large pot over medium-high heat. Add 1 tablespoon of the EVOO and the butter. Once the butter has melted and the pot is hot, add the ground chicken. Brown it, using the back of a wooden spoon to break it up into small pieces, about 5 to 6 minutes. ■ Add the carrot, onions, celery, garlic, paprika, bay leaf, and some salt and pepper. Cook, stirring frequently, for 3 to 4 minutes. ■ Add the chicken stock and scrape up any brown bits on the bottom of the pot. Add the hot sauce and tomato sauce, and bring up to a bubble. Simmer for 8 to 10 minutes to let the flavors come together. ■ While the chili is simmering, take the potatoes out of the oven and slice the top third off so the potato resembles a boat. Gently scoop the potato pulp out of the skins, reserving it in a bowl. ■ To the bowl with the potato pulp, add the blue cheese, egg, sour cream, the whites of the scallions, and salt and pepper. Gently mix to combine. ■ Fill the hollowed-out potato skins with the potato mixture. Place them into the oven for 10 minutes, until nice and hot. ■ To serve, place a stuffed potato onto a plate and top it with some buffalo chicken chili (be sure to discard the bay leaf). Garnish with the sliced scallion greens.

grilled shrimp with chili cocktail sauce

Combine the first seven ingredients in a bowl and season with pepper to taste, then chill. ■ Heat a grill pan or grill to medium-high. ■ Dress the shrimp with the EVOO, paprika, and salt and pepper. Skewer the shrimp on metal skewers to help in turning them and grill until the shrimp are opaque and firm, 7 to 8 minutes. Pile the shrimp on a platter and pour the sauce over or pass the sauce at the table. Garnish with the parsley.

SERVES 4

⅔ to ¾ cup **chili sauce**

2 tablespoons **prepared horseradish**

2 tablespoons **lemon juice** (juice of ½ lemon)

1 tablespoon **hot sauce** (eyeball it)

2 teaspoons **Worcestershire sauce**

1 teaspoon **celery seed**, ⅓ palmful

1 **celery stalk** from the heart with leafy tops, finely chopped

Coarse black pepper

16 **jumbo shrimp**, peeled and deveined

2 tablespoons **EVOO** (extra-virgin olive oil)

1 teaspoon **sweet smoked paprika**

Salt

A small handful of fresh **flat-leaf parsley** leaves, finely chopped, for garnish

blt bruschetta

6 to 8 slices **bacon**, chopped

1 loaf crusty **Italian bread**

3 ripe **Hass avocados**, pitted and peeled

Juice of 1 **lemon**, divided

Salt and **pepper**

1 large **garlic clove**, mashed into a paste

2 pints **heirloom tomatoes**, chopped

1 handful of **arugula**, chopped

4 sprigs of fresh **tarragon**, leaves removed and chopped

1½ cups fresh **basil** leaves, chopped

3 tablespoons **EVOO** (extra-virgin olive oil)

Preheat the grill or broiler. ■ Heat a large skillet over medium-low heat. Add the bacon and cook until crispy. Drain on a paper-towel-lined plate and reserve. ■ Slice the bread about an inch thick. Char the bread on both sides on the grill or under the broiler. Remove and reserve. ■ In a medium-size mixing bowl, mash up the avocado with half of the lemon juice, salt and pepper, and the mashed garlic, then spread some avocado mash onto each piece of charred sliced bread. ■ In another mixing bowl, combine the chopped tomatoes with the arugula, tarragon, basil, salt and pepper, the reserved bacon, the remaining lemon juice, and the EVOO. Top each of the avocado-smeared bread slices with some of the tomato, bacon, and arugula mixture.

tomato stacks

1 tablespoon **EVOO** (extra-virgin olive oil)

6 slices **bacon**, chopped

½ cup **buttermilk**

1 cup **crème fraîche**

1 **garlic clove**, grated

2 tablespoons chopped fresh **dill**

2 tablespoons chopped fresh **chives**

Juice of 1 **lemon**

3 to 4 tablespoons **prepared horseradish**

Salt and **pepper**

6 **beefsteak tomatoes**

1 small **red onion**, thinly sliced into rings

Place a small skillet over medium heat with the EVOO. Add the chopped bacon to the skillet and cook until golden and crispy, about 5 minutes. Remove the bacon to a paper-towel-lined plate and let cool. ■ While the bacon is cooking, whisk together the buttermilk, crème fraîche, garlic, dill, chives, lemon juice, horseradish, and salt and pepper in a medium mixing bowl. Set the dressing aside. ■ Slice each of the tomatoes in half widthwise. Lay a few rings of red onion onto the base of each tomato and then cap each tomato off with its top. Transfer the tomato stacks to a serving plate, top with a little of the prepared dressing, and garnish with the bacon.

5 yes! the kids will eat it

4 30-minu meals

6 sides & starte

7 simple sauces & bottom-of-the-jar tips

Use these gravies and simple sauces to top chicken breasts or pork chops. Each recipe will provide enough sauce for up to 4 portions. For chicken breasts or chops, season with salt and pepper and cook the meat in a nonstick skillet—12 minutes for boneless skinless chicken and 8 minutes for 1-inch-thick chops, turning once. Bottom-of-the-jar recipes help you use up the last of many refrigerator-door staples, to find every last bit of value in your grocery dollars.

8 desserts

simple pan sauces

Make one of these sauces in the hot skillet after you have cooked chicken breasts or pork chops.

barbecue gravy

3 tablespoons **butter**

3 tablespoons all-purpose **flour**

2 cups **chicken stock**

¼ cup **barbecue sauce**

Salt and **pepper**

Remove the cooked chicken or pork from the skillet. Working over medium-high heat, add the butter, swish it around the pan to melt it, then whisk in the flour and cook until light brown, about 1 minute. Whisk in the chicken stock and barbecue sauce and season with salt and pepper. Continue whisking and cook until thickened, about 3 minutes. Pour the sauce over the chicken or pork.

apple cider gravy

3 tablespoons **butter**

3 tablespoons all-purpose **flour**

2 cups **chicken stock**

½ cup **apple cider**

Salt and **pepper**

Remove the cooked chicken or pork from the skillet. Working over medium-high heat, add the butter, swish it around the pan to melt it, then whisk in the flour and cook until light brown, about 1 minute. Whisk in the chicken stock and apple cider and season with salt and pepper. Continue whisking and cook until thickened, about 3 minutes. Pour the sauce over the chicken or pork.

creamy grainy mustard gravy

⅔ cup **chicken stock**

⅓ cup **heavy cream**

2 heaping tablespoons **grainy mustard**

Salt and **pepper**

Remove the cooked chicken or pork from the skillet. Working over medium-high heat, add the chicken stock, heavy cream, and grainy mustard to the pan. Bring up to a bubble and simmer until thickened enough to coat the back of a spoon, 3 to 4 minutes. Season with salt and pepper and pour over the chicken or pork.

cider pan gravy

Remove the cooked chicken or pork from the skillet. Place a medium pot over medium-high heat with the butter. Sprinkle the flour over the melted butter and cook for about 1 minute. Whisk the stock and cider into the mixture and bring up to a bubble. Add the mustard and the thyme, then season with salt and pepper. Simmer until thickened, 4 to 5 minutes. ■ Serve warm over your favorite meat or stuffing and/or side dish.

3 tablespoons **butter**

2 tablespoons all-purpose **flour**

1 cup **chicken stock**

½ cup **apple cider**

1 tablespoon **grainy mustard**

3 to 4 sprigs of fresh **thyme**, leaves removed and chopped

Salt and **pepper**

orange-maple sauce

Remove the cooked chicken or pork from the skillet. Turn the heat under the skillet to high, then add the chicken stock, orange juice, maple syrup, and red pepper flakes together. Let the mixture come to a bubble and reduce by half, until thick and syrupy, about 5 minutes. Season the sauce with salt and pepper. Pour the sauce over the chicken or pork.

½ cup **chicken stock**

½ cup **orange juice**

¼ cup **maple syrup**

Pinch of **crushed red pepper flakes** or chili powder

Salt and **pepper**

tarragon mustard sauce

Remove the cooked chicken or pork from the skillet. Working over medium-high heat, add the chicken stock, heavy cream, mustard, and tarragon. Bring up to a bubble and simmer until thickened enough to coat the back of a spoon, 3 to 4 minutes. Season with salt and pepper and pour over the cooked chicken or pork.

⅔ cup **chicken stock**

⅓ cup **heavy cream**

2 tablespoons **Dijon mustard**

2 stems fresh **tarragon**, leaves removed and chopped

Salt and **pepper**

lemon-thyme sauce

2 tablespoons **butter**

4 sprigs of fresh **thyme**, leaves removed and roughly chopped

1 **shallot**, chopped

1 rounded tablespoon all-purpose **flour**

1½ cups **chicken stock**

1 **lemon**

Salt and **pepper**

Remove the cooked chicken or pork from the skillet. Working over medium-high heat, melt the butter, add the thyme and shallot, and cook for about 2 minutes. Sprinkle the flour into the pan, then cook for 1 minute. Whisk in the chicken stock, bring it up to a bubble, and cook until thickened, 2 minutes. Add 2 teaspoons of lemon zest and the juice of the zested lemon, and season with salt and pepper. Pour the sauce over the chicken or pork and serve.

curry sauce

2 tablespoons **butter**

1 small **onion**, finely chopped

½ small **Granny Smith apple**, peeled, cored, and thinly sliced

1 heaping tablespoon **curry powder**

1 rounded tablespoon all-purpose **flour**

1½ cups **chicken stock**

¼ cup **mango chutney**

Salt and **pepper**

Remove the cooked chicken or pork from the skillet. Working over medium-high heat, melt the butter, add the onions, and cook, stirring every now and then, for 3 to 4 minutes. Add the apples and curry powder and continue to cook for another 3 to 4 minutes. Sprinkle the flour into the pan, cook for 1 minute, then whisk in the chicken stock and stir in the chutney. Season the sauce with salt and pepper and simmer for 2 to 3 minutes. Top the chicken or pork with the sauce.

no-cook sauces for chicken

lemon-dijon sauce

In a medium-size mixing bowl, whisk together the lemon juice, parsley, capers, mustard, and salt and pepper. Slowly drizzle in the EVOO while whisking until combined. Pour over a sautéed chicken breast for an instant sauce!

Juice of 1 **lemon**

2 tablespoons finely chopped fresh **flat-leaf parsley** leaves

2 tablespoons **capers**, drained

1 tablespoon **Dijon mustard**

Salt and **pepper**

¼ cup **EVOO** (extra-virgin olive oil)

pineapple-ginger sauce

In a medium-size mixing bowl, whisk together all ingredients. Pour over a sautéed chicken breast for an instant sauce!

1 (15-ounce) can **crushed pineapple**, no sugar added

2 tablespoons **tamari** (aged soy sauce)

½ inch of fresh **gingerroot**, peeled and grated

3 **scallions**, sliced

apple cider marinade

2 cups **apple cider**

Zest and juice of 1 **lemon**

2 tablespoons **Dijon mustard**

3 to 4 sprigs of fresh **thyme**, leaves removed and chopped

3 to 4 tablespoons **EVOO** (extra-virgin olive oil)

Salt and **pepper**

2 pounds of your favorite cut of **meat**, such as chicken breast or pork chops

In a large resealable plasic bag or shallow casserole dish, combine the cider, lemon zest and juice, mustard, thyme, EVOO, and salt and pepper. Add the meat to the marinade and refrigerate for at least 2 hours and up to overnight. Remove the meat from the marinade and prepare the meat to your liking. Discard the marinade.

bottom-of-the-jar tips

bottom of the jar
pickled vegetables and brie

1 small round of **Brie**, 4 to 5 inches in diameter

Various **bottoms of jars**, such as olives, pickled vegetables, capers, roasted red peppers, sweet or hot pepper rings

Sliced **baguette** or whole-grain bread

Cut the top rind off of the Brie. Place the cheese on a microwave-safe plate and microwave on high for about 1 minute. While the cheese is in the microwave, chop the bottom-of-the-jar item or items. Use up to ½ cup of any mix of pickled items. Remove the warm cheese from the microwave and top with the chopped vegetables. Spread on the bread and enjoy!

4 APPETIZER-SIZE PORTIONS

bottom of the jar
salsa dressing

This makes a great dressing for a Tex-Mex salad. It also spices up pork, chicken, or fish when added to the pan at the end of cooking, and it makes a zippy drizzle for finished sides!

Add the EVOO, vinegar, salt, and pepper to the salsa jar and give it a good shake.

MAKES ¾ TO 1 CUP

⅓ cup **EVOO** (extra-virgin olive oil)

¼ cup **vinegar** of choice

Salt and **pepper**

Bottom of the jar of **salsa**, a couple of tablespoons to ¼ cup

bottom of the jar
asian-style glaze

In the marmalade jar combine the tamari, garlic, and ginger and shake until completely incorporated. Pour over any skillet-cooked meat right before it's done and continue to cook until the glaze thickens, 2 minutes.

MAKES ½ CUP

Bottom of the jar of **marmalade**, up to 2 tablespoons

2 tablespoons **tamari** (aged soy sauce)

1 small **garlic clove**, finely chopped or grated

1 inch of fresh **gingerroot**, peeled and grated

bottom of the jar
spicy thai peanut sauce

Use the sauce as a dip for chicken tenders. Or pour over 1 pound warm whole-wheat noodles and garnish with toasted sesame seeds and chopped scallions.

Loosen the peanut butter in the jar by microwaving it, with the lid off, for 30 seconds on high. Add the water, tamari, lime zest and juice, and red pepper flakes to the jar. Screw the lid on and shake to combine.

MAKES ⅔ CUP

Bottom of the jar of **peanut butter**, 3 to 4 tablespoons

3 tablespoons **hot water**

3 tablespoons **tamari** (aged soy sauce)

Zest and juice of 1 **lime**

1 teaspoon **crushed red pepper flakes**

bottom of the jar
orange bourbon glaze

¼ cup **bourbon**

Bottom of the jar of **orange marmalade**, up to 2 tablespoons

Use this glaze to liven up sautéed chicken or pork.

Pour the bourbon into the marmalade jar and shake until completely incorporated. Remove the cooked meat from the skillet and pour the glaze into the pan. Then return the glaze to the heat and stand back as it will flame up if you are using a gas burner. Continue to cook until the flame dies down and the glaze thickens, 2 minutes.

MAKES ENOUGH GLAZE FOR 4 PORTIONS OF CHICKEN OR PORK

bottom of the jar
pickle-mustard dressing

3 tablespoons **pickle juice**

Bottom of the jar of **Dijon mustard**, 1 tablespoon

1 small **shallot**, finely chopped

Salt and **pepper**

¼ cup **EVOO** (extra-virgin olive oil)

1 tablespoon chopped fresh **flat-leaf parsley** or basil leaves, chives, or dill

Use this dressing for 4 to 6 servings or to dress a 1-pound sack of slaw salad mix.

Pour the pickle juice into the mustard jar; add the shallots and some salt and pepper. Screw on the lid and shake vigorously. To be extra careful, wrap a paper towel around the lid before shaking. Remove the lid and pour into a salad bowl, then whisk in the EVOO and your herb of choice.

MAKES ¾ CUP

bottom of the container
pound cake with dessert sauce

Melt the sorbet or ice cream for 20 seconds on high in the microwave. In the bottom of the ice cream container, mash 5 or 6 strawberries, raspberries, and blackberries with a fork until combined. Add the nip of liqueur, replace the container top, and give it a good shake. ■ Slice the cake into 8 pieces and cut each slice into 3 sticks. Divide the cake pieces equally among 8 dessert cups or martini glasses. Spoon the sauce over the cake, top with the remaining berries and with whipped cream, and garnish with lime zest.

SERVES 8

Bottom of the container of **fruit sorbet** or of vanilla or chocolate ice cream, up to ½ cup

1 pint **strawberries**, hulled and chopped

½ pint **raspberries**

½ pint **blackberries**

A nip of **orange liqueur**, such as Grand Marnier, 2 ounces

1 **pound cake**

Whipped cream

Zest of 1 **lime**

bottom of the drawer
mustard-soy dipping sauce

Serve with store-bought cooked egg rolls, pot stickers, or chicken tenders.

Combine the soy sauce, duck sauce, and mustard in a small mixing bowl and whisk together.

MAKES ¼ CUP

2 packets **soy sauce**

3 packets **duck sauce**

1 packet **hot mustard**

bottom of the drawer
sweet-and-sour dipping sauce

This is a terrific dressing for cucumber salad. Toss with 1 thinly sliced peeled seedless cucumber and 1 thinly sliced shallot or ¼ red onion.

Combine the duck sauce, vinegar, red pepper flakes, and water in a small mixing bowl and whisk together.

MAKES ⅓ CUP

4 packets **duck sauce**

2 tablespoons **rice wine vinegar** or white wine vinegar

½ teaspoon **crushed red pepper flakes**

1 tablespoon **water**

bottom of the cereal box
dessert parfait

½ cup **mixed berries**

½ cup **vanilla yogurt**

¼ cup **cereal crumbs** from the bottom of the box

In a small serving glass, layer the ingredients beginning with the berries, yogurt, cereal, then repeat.

1 SERVING

bottom of the jar
peanut butter–chocolate sauce

Bottom of the jar of **peanut butter**, up to ¼ cup

½ cup **chocolate sauce**

2 to 3 tablespoons **hot water**

3 tablespoons **chopped peanuts**

In the bottom of a peanut butter jar, add the chocolate sauce, hot water, and chopped nuts. Screw the lid back on the jar and give the mixture a good shimmy-shake until everything is combined. Pour the sauce over your favorite ice cream or cake.

MAKES 1 CUP

bottom of the jar
peanut butter–caramel sauce

Bottom of the jar of **peanut butter**, up to ¼ cup

½ cup **caramel sauce**

2 to 3 tablespoons **hot water**

2 tablespoons **orange liqueur**, such as Grand Marnier (optional)

In the bottom of a peanut butter jar, add the caramel sauce, hot water, and orange liqueur. Screw the lid back on the jar and give the mixture a good shimmy-shake until everything is combined. Pour the sauce over your favorite ice cream or cake. Yum-o!

MAKES 1 CUP

8 desserts

I do not bake, because I am competitive and I know baking is just not my forte. Plus, baking is more of a science than a purely creative art, and I stink at science! Still, I do have a few easy dessert solutions to share, and here they are. This section is thin, but I'm proud of these sweet little treats, and I am trying to better my baking skills and myself. I'm working on my flour and sugar karma. Look for future sweet sections of my books to be thicker, perhaps. I am off to a good start. I actually made my mom's éclairs from scratch this past year and they were close to perfect and divinely delicious. See page 310 for the recipe.

easiest-ever
baked stuffed apples

6 firm fresh-picked **apples**

½ **lemon**

4 tablespoons (½ stick) **butter**, softened

1 cup **muesli cereal** with dried fruit

4 tablespoons **dark brown sugar**

½ cup chopped **walnuts**

2 teaspoons grated orange or lemon **zest**

1 teaspoon ground **ginger**

1 teaspoon ground **cinnamon**

½ teaspoon freshly grated **nutmeg**

2 pints **vanilla bean ice cream**

Preheat the oven to 425°F. ▪ Trim the tops of the apples and scoop out the center and seeds with a small melon baller. Wipe the edges of the trimmed fruit with lemon. Combine the butter, cereal, sugar, nuts, citrus zest, and spices and then fill the apples. Set the apples upright in a baking dish or muffin tin and bake for 20 to 25 minutes, until tender. Top with ice cream and serve hot.

green melon with
lime & lemon sorbet

1 **honeydew melon**, seeded and quartered

Zest and juice of 1 **lime**

A handful of fresh **mint leaves**, chopped

1 pint **lemon sorbet**

Dress the melon quarters with lime zest and juice and mint. Fill each quarter with a small scoop of lemon sorbet and serve.

small strawberries
with lemon

Toss the berries in a bowl with the lemon juice and sugar and let stand for a few minutes. Toss with the mint and serve.

SERVES 4

2 pints small **strawberries**, whole or halved, stemmed and hulled

Juice of 1 **lemon**

2 teaspoons **sugar**

A handful of fresh **mint leaves**, torn or shredded

limoncello & lemon
cream fruit tart

Remove the tart shell from its packaging and place on a cake plate. Douse the cake with the limoncello. Whisk or beat together the cream, mascarpone cheese, lemon curd, and lemon zest in a large bowl to combine. Fill the tart shell and top with the berries and mint.

SERVES 6

1 (12-inch) store-bought **sponge cake tart shell**, available in the produce or bakery section

2 ounces chilled **limoncello** liqueur

1 cup **heavy cream**

1 cup **mascarpone cheese**

⅓ cup **lemon curd**

2 teaspoons grated **lemon zest**

½ pint **raspberries**

½ pint **blackberries**

2 tablespoons fresh **mint leaves**, very thinly sliced

berries with
almond cream & amaretti

2 pints **strawberries**, hulled and halved

2 ounces **Grand Marnier** or another orange-flavored liqueur

3 tablespoons **sugar**

1 cup **whipping cream**

1 teaspoon **almond extract**

12 **amaretti cookies**, unwrapped and lightly crushed

In a medium bowl, douse the berries in the Grand Marnier and sprinkle with a tablespoon of the sugar. Let the berries hang out to get their juices flowing. ■ Beat the cream with the remaining 2 tablespoons of sugar and the almond extract until the whipped cream forms peaks. ■ Serve the berries with whipped cream and amaretti for topping.

black pepper–
cinnamon honey
with fruit & ice cream

1 cup **honey**

1 teaspoon **coarse black pepper**

1 **cinnamon stick**

2 cups chopped or sliced **apricots**, plums, peaches, or pineapple

2 pints **vanilla bean ice cream**

Rolled or **wafer cookies**, for garnish

Heat the honey in a small pot over low heat with the pepper and cinnamon stick. When ready to serve, toss the honey with the fruit and spill it over the ice cream in dessert dishes. Garnish with the cookies.

strawberry-balsamic
lemonade

Place the berries and vinegar in the bottom of a glass pitcher, then muddle with a wooden spoon. ■ Dissolve the sugar in ⅔ cup of the water over medium heat, then pour over the strawberries. ■ Juice the lemons and add to the pitcher. Fill the pitcher with the remaining 5⅓ cups of water and stir. Chill or pour over ice and the torn mint leaves and serve.

SERVES 4

1 pint small **strawberries**, hulled and halved

1 tablespoon **aged balsamic vinegar**

⅓ cup **sugar**

6 cups still or sparkling **mineral water**

12 **lemons**

A few sprigs of **fresh mint**, torn

mulled cran-cider

Steep the juice, ginger, orange peel, cinnamon, cloves, and cider and keep warm in a pot over low heat. Strain the cider as you serve and garnish with a few cranberries if desired.

SERVES 6

2 cups all-natural **cranberry juice**

1 inch of fresh **gingerroot**, peeled

A long curl of **orange peel**

1 **cinnamon stick**

2 whole **cloves**

1 quart **apple cider**, the cloudy kind

1 cup **whole cranberries**, for garnish (optional)

peanut butter
hot chocolate
with vanilla whipped cream

SERVES 6

1 cup **heavy cream**

1 tablespoon **sugar**

1 teaspoon **vanilla extract**

6 cups **whole milk**

1 split **vanilla bean**

1 **cinnamon stick**

6 ounces **bittersweet chocolate,** grated

2 tablespoons **creamy peanut butter**

In a large mixing bowl, whisk the cream, sugar, and vanilla to make whipped cream, 3 to 4 minutes, then chill. Bring the milk, vanilla bean, and cinnamon stick to a simmer in a large saucepan, then whisk in the chocolate and peanut butter. Reduce the heat and simmer for a few minutes, remove from the heat, discard the vanilla bean and cinnamon stick, and cover to keep hot. Serve the peanut butter hot chocolate with whipped cream on top.

italian
spumoni towers

SERVES 3

12 slices store-bought **pound cake** (each ¼ to ½ inch thick)

1 pint **chocolate ice cream**

1 pint **pistachio ice cream**

1 pint **strawberry or cherry ice cream**

Chocolate sauce

Using a round cookie cutter or small can, trim the sliced pound cake into disks. Layer, starting with a slice of pound cake, then a small scoop of chocolate ice cream, a slice of pound cake, then pistachio ice cream, a slice of pound cake, and strawberry ice cream, finishing with a slice of pound cake to form spumoni towers. Individually wrap and freeze to set. To serve, place on a rack set over a baking sheet, and pour sauce over top to cover. Transfer to dessert plates and serve.

fall fruit
individual crostatas

These can be served as individual open-faced pie slices.

Preheat the oven to 400°F. Arrange 2 racks near the center of the oven. ■ Combine the apples, cranberries, and pears in a bowl. Toss with the lemon juice, cornstarch, brown sugar, cinnamon, nutmeg, cloves or allspice, ginger, and salt. ■ Roll the dough out a bit on a lightly floured surface. Cut each pie crust into 4 large wedges. Cover 2 baking sheets with parchment paper and arrange 4 wedges on each sheet. Arrange one eighth of the fruit mixture on each wedge. Fold the edges of each wedge in about an inch, leaving the filling in the center of each wedge exposed. Dot the exposed fruit with the butter and brush the exposed crust with the egg wash. Bake for 12 to 15 minutes, until golden, then cool on racks for 10 minutes. Serve warm.

SERVES 8

2 Empire, Gala, or Honey Crisp **apples**, peeled, cored, and sliced

¼ cup **dried sweetened cranberries**

2 slightly underripe **brown-skinned pears**, peeled, cored, and thinly sliced

2 teaspoons **lemon juice**

1 tablespoon **cornstarch**

3 tablespoons **brown sugar**

¼ teaspoon ground **cinnamon**

Pinch of freshly grated **nutmeg**

Pinch of ground **cloves** or allspice

Pinch of ground **ginger**

Pinch of **salt**

2 store-bought **pie crusts** (rolled, not in pie pans)

All-purpose **flour**, for rolling the dough

2 tablespoons cold **butter**, cut into small pieces

1 **egg**, beaten with a splash of water

banana-sicles

1 cup **strawberry preserves**

4 **bananas**, peeled and cut in half widthwise

8 **Popsicle sticks**

¾ cup **granola**, any kind your kids like

¾ cup **walnuts**, or any kind of nuts you like

Heat the preserves in a high-sided bowl in the microwave until they thin out. Pierce each banana half through the center of the cut side with a Popsicle stick. Dip the bananas into the strawberry preserves until they're completely coated. ■ Place the granola and nuts on separate plates. After dipping a banana into the preserves, coat it in the nuts or granola, whichever you prefer. Make the coating stick to the banana by pressing lightly on the coating with your hands. Place the coated bananas on a small baking sheet lined with wax paper and pop them into the freezer until ready to eat.

grasshopper brownies

Nonstick cooking spray

1 box **brownie mix**

2 **eggs**, or as many as needed for the mix

4 tablespoons **oil**, or as much as needed for the mix

1 cup chopped **chocolate-mint candy**, such as Andes

1 cup **crushed chocolate sandwich cookies**, such as Oreos

Preheat the oven to the temperature indicated on the box. Line a baking dish with parchment paper or aluminum foil and spray it well with cooking spray. ■ Prepare the brownies according to the package directions, using eggs and oil as directed. Stir half of the candy into the batter. Transfer to the baking dish and sprinkle the remaining candy and the crushed cookies over the top. ■ Bake according to the package directions, until a toothpick inserted in the center comes out clean. Cool completely before cutting. ■ Heads up: Cutting these guys gets a lot easier if you refrigerate them once they're cool—and they're also deliciously fudgy when served cold!

individual strawberry
shortcake ice cream cups

Line a muffin tin with plastic wrap. You will only use 6 of the cups.
■ Slice the pound cake widthwise into twelve ¼-inch-thick slices.
Using a 5-ounce can (a small tomato paste can works well), cut
6 circles out of 6 slices of cake. With the remaining 6 slices, use a
15-ounce can to make 6 slightly larger circles of cake for the tops.
You should end up with 6 small circles and 6 large circles. ■ Put the
small circles of cake on the bottom of each of the 6 individual muffin
cups. Then, line each muffin cup with slices of strawberries to create
a wall. You now should have 6 individual holders lined at the bottom
with cake and along the sides with strawberries. Fill each cake cup
with a scoop of ice cream and place the larger circles of cake on top
to form lids. Wrap the whole tin in plastic wrap and place in the
freezer for at least an hour to firm up. ■ To serve, gently lift each
individual ice cream cake out of the tin, using the plastic wrap to
help them release. Place each cake upside down on a dessert plate.
Drizzle melted strawberry sorbet over the cake.

MAKES 6 INDIVIDUAL
ICE CREAM CAKES

1 **pound cake**, flavor of your choice

1 pint **strawberries**, hulled and
sliced ¼ inch thick

1 pint **French vanilla ice cream**,
slightly softened

1 cup melted **strawberry sorbet**

éclairs

PASTRY CREAM

¾ cup **sugar**

Pinch of **salt**

3¼ cups **milk**

¼ cup **cornstarch**

3 **egg yolks**

2 teaspoons **vanilla extract**

ÉCLAIR DOUGH

6 tablespoons (¾ stick) **butter**

About ½ teaspoon **salt**

1 cup all-purpose **flour**

4 **eggs**

CHOCOLATE ICING

6 ounces **semisweet or bittersweet chocolate**, finely chopped, approximately 1 cup

½ cup **heavy cream**

MAKE THE PASTRY CREAM: In a medium sauce pot over medium heat, combine the sugar, salt, and 3 cups of the milk, and bring up to a bubble. While the milk is heating up, combine the remaining ¼ cup of milk with the cornstarch in a bowl and stir until completely dissolved. In another large bowl, break up the egg yolks and whisk them together. ■ Using a whisk, add the cornstarch mixture to the simmering milk and stir continuously until thickened, about 2 minutes (it's OK if the mixture comes to a low boil). ■ When the mixture has thickened, slowly add a couple ladlefuls of the hot liquid to the bowl with the egg yolks while whisking constantly. Add the egg yolk mixture back to the pot, return it to medium heat, and simmer until thickened, about 2 minutes. Remove the pot from the heat and stir in the vanilla extract. ■ Transfer the mixture to a bowl and cover with plastic wrap, pushing the plastic down so that it covers the surface of the cream to prevent a skin from forming. Refrigerate until chilled, at least 2 hours and up to overnight.

MAKE THE PASTRY: Preheat the oven to 400°F. ■ In a medium sauce pot over medium-high heat, combine 1 cup water, the butter, and salt. Heat until the butter has melted and the water is boiling. ■ Add the flour and cook, stirring constantly with a wooden spoon, until the mixture begins to create a dough ball in the center of the pot and the dough is completely pulling away from the sides of the pan, about 2 minutes. ■ Transfer the mixture to a mixing bowl or the bowl of a stand mixer fitted with a paddle attachment. On low speed, add the eggs to the mixture one at a time, scraping the sides of the bowl well after each addition and beating until the bowl feels cool (the mixture should be very smooth and silky). ■ Transfer the mixture to a plastic food-storage bag and cut ½ inch off of one corner to create a pastry bag. On a baking sheet lined with parchment paper, pipe out about sixteen 4-inch-long lines of dough to make small éclairs. Leave about 2 inches of space between each éclair. Bake until golden brown and puffed, about 40 minutes. ■ The pastries can be made a day or two ahead of time and kept in an airtight container at room temperature. If they feel soggy when you take them out, pop them into a 400°F oven for a couple of minutes until they crisp up again. Allow them to cool before filling.

MAKE THE CHOCOLATE ICING: Place the chopped chocolate in a small to medium-size stainless-steel or glass mixing bowl and set aside. Heat the cream in a small sauce pot over medium heat and carefully bring to a boil. Be careful; the cream can burn quickly. Remove the cream from the heat and pour it over the chocolate in the bowl. Immediately start stirring to fully incorporate the chocolate. Stir until it is melted. Cool the chocolate slightly before using. ■ To assemble the éclairs, give the pastry cream a stir and smooth it out, then transfer it to a plastic food-storage bag. Cut off about ¼ inch from one corner to make a pastry bag. ■ Using a chopstick or the tip of a pair of scissors, poke a hole in one end of each baked pastry. Squeeze the pastry cream into each opening, filling the pastries. To finish, spoon about 1 tablespoon of the warm icing across the top of each éclair or dip the top of each éclair in the icing. Serve immediately or refrigerate until ready to serve. You may spread a simple chocolate frosting on top instead of the melted chocolate if you'd like.

cone-noli

In a mixing bowl, combine the ricotta, cream cheese, and powdered sugar and set aside. ■ Drop a few strawberries into the bottom of each sugar cone. Spoon some of the sweetened ricotta on top of the strawberries and sprinkle the tops with the mini chocolate chips.

SERVES 6

2 cups **ricotta cheese**

1 (8-ounce) package **cream cheese**, at room temperature

¼ cup **powdered sugar**

6 **sugar cones**

1 cup **strawberries**, hulled and quartered

½ cup **mini chocolate chips**

margarita
ice pops

SERVES 6

3 cups **limeade**

3 tablespoons **tequila**

3 tablespoons **Grand Marnier** liqueur

Kosher salt, for garnish

Mix the ingredients together in a pitcher or measuring cup and pour into ice pop molds. Freeze for 4 to 5 hours. ■ Dip the molds in hot water to release the pops. ■ Sprinkle the pops with salt before serving.

banana "ice cream"
fake-out

SERVES 4

3 **bananas**, peeled and cut into chunks, frozen

¼ cup **milk**

In the bowl of a food processor, puree the frozen bananas, adding the milk in small increments as needed to loosen the mixture, until whipped, about 2 minutes. ■ Serve the "ice cream" immediately with your favorite toppings.

root beer float granita

SERVES 4

1 (12-ounce) bottle of **root beer**, brand of choice

1 pint **vanilla ice cream**

Pour the root beer into a shallow pan and place in the freezer. Freeze for 5 to 6 hours or overnight. Once the mixture is frozen, scrape it with a fork to make shaved ice flakes. Serve scoops of vanilla ice cream in 4 cups or bowls and top with the root beer granita.

fake-out cheesecake

In a bowl, combine the cream cheese with the orange and lemon zests. Using a rubber spatula, beat in the ricotta cheese and powdered sugar. Divide the cheese mixture among the 4 individual graham cracker crusts, top each one with some of the sliced strawberries, and chill for up to 30 minutes or overnight.

SERVES 4

4 ounces **cream cheese**, at room temperature

Zest of 1 **orange**

Zest of 1 **lemon**

1 cup **whole-milk ricotta cheese**

¼ cup **powdered sugar**

4 individual **graham cracker crusts**

8 **strawberries**, sliced

apple cider cake with cinnamon cream cheese frosting

Swap cider for the liquid (water or milk) in your favorite golden cake mix and make a cake or cupcakes. Top with the cinnamon cream cheese frosting.

In the bowl of an electric mixer fitted with the paddle attachment or in a large mixing bowl with a handheld mixer, beat together the cream cheese, butter, powdered sugar, vanilla, and cinnamon until smooth and creamy, 4 to 5 minutes.

SERVES 6 TO 8

1 (8-ounce) package **cream cheese**, at room temperature

4 tablespoons (½ stick) **butter**, at room temperature

3 cups **powdered sugar**

1 teaspoon **vanilla extract**

2 teaspoons ground **cinnamon**

index